PREFACE

In this study of suggestion, in relation to statement, in English poetry, I have started by examining 'Suggestion'—the term and the concept: sketching its origin and development and indicating its present status. I have proceeded, in the third, fourth and fifth chapters, to consider the two kinds into which suggestion can be divided: the suggestion of emotion, and suggestion through metaphor. The sixth and seventh chapters, to be read with the fourth, analyse suggestion and statement in relation to each other. Two case studies follow: T. S. Eliot and Wordsworth. We next revert to character and plot as objective correlatives. The concluding chapter touches upon certain problems of suggested meaning, such as: Should it be evaluated? When is it paraphrasable? What happens when it is defined or explicated?

I have constantly brought in concepts from Sanskrit poetics, but invariably as points of departure for discussion of poetic practice and critical ideas in English. If at certain points the book sounds like special pleading for Sanskrit theory, I can only say that that, at any rate, was not my intention. This essay is not an exposition of Sanskrit poetics, nor is it a comparative study of Sanskrit and English critical theory—anything in that line will have to await the advent of the super-scholar who matches a knowledge of what the ninth-to-eleventh-century Indian theorists of poetry meant with a specifically modern sensibility and equipment which can enable him to work at a deeper level than that of seeming affinities and to speak a language which will not distort what those masters said and yet will be comprehensible to present-day English-speaking readers.

In citing the work of other critics I suspect that I may be charged with having drawn upon too small a company and then on too few of their writings—Abercrombie, Tillyard, Richards, Empson, Eliot, Cleanth Brooks, Wimsatt, and John Bayley. Here is a selection at least part of which will be felt to be either old-fashioned or eccentric. But if certain critical works seemed to offer more ideas than others, serving as useful points of departure, I saw no reason why I should not make use of them freely.

There are other and more considerable debts owed to those whose support and advice made this book possible: F. W. Bateson, Bruce Pattison, Harold Osborne, Robin Skelton and Krishna Arjunwadkar.

K. R.

Suggestion and Statement
in Poetry

Suggestion
and Statement
in Poetry

KRISHNA RAYAN

UNIVERSITY OF LONDON
THE ATHLONE PRESS
1972

Published by
THE ATHLONE PRESS
UNIVERSITY OF LONDON
at 4 Gower Street, London WC1
Distributed by Tiptree Book Services Ltd
Tiptree, Essex

0 485 11134 9

T C

Printed in Great Britain by
T. & A. CONSTABLE LTD
EDINBURGH

ACKNOWLEDGEMENTS

I am grateful to the editors and publishers of the following journals for permission to reprint material originally published in them (date of numbers is shown in brackets): *Essays in Criticism* for Chapter 8 (July 1969) and part of Chapter 9 (October 1967); *British Journal of Aesthetics* for part of Chapter 2 (January 1969) and Chapter 3 (July 1965); *Malahat Review* for Chapter 5 (April 1967), Chapter 6 (April 1970) and part of Chapter 11 (July 1968).

Acknowledgement is also made to the following for use of copyright material as specified in detail in the relevant notes: Faber and Faber Ltd for extracts from poems by Thom Gunn and Robert Lowell; Granada Publishing Ltd for extracts from poems by R. S. Thomas; the Longman Group Ltd for a poem by Patricia Beer; Macmillan and Co. Ltd for a poem by W. B. Yeats; Routledge and Kegan Paul Ltd for a poem by John Holloway.

K. R.

CONTENTS

1

Suggestion Today

Finding that the fallen trees obstruct the view, you leave the main path and advance to the open cliff edge where a close-up of the Victoria Falls must be easy to have. As you approach the coign, however, you see a giant cloud of spray climbing out of the gorge, and the next moment you are blinking at a grey impenetrable wall that has obliterated everything. Nevertheless, the Falls are a commanding presence, for through the barrier of spray you can hear a muffled roar, and you know that the massed waters are tumbling into the gorge at your feet. The evidence of your ears affirms that the Victoria Falls are there before you, but their identity is indeterminate, ambiguous and obliquely apprehended—you are aware that behind the spray it can either be an angry torrent gushing through a constriction, or a stately wall of water; it can either be a row of shrunken streams, or a single undiminished expanse. The first man to be able to define this apprehension of the Zambesi's veiled descent was a local Lozi whose nomenclatory imagination called the Falls *Musi-o-tunya*, 'the Smoke that Thunders'.

Here in this sightless instant—you tell yourself as you retreat before the drenching spray back to the main path—is held an experience that uniquely projects the whole process of poetic suggestion. Like the Falls, the suggested meaning waits beyond the frontiers of the overt and the explicit, unseen but powerfully felt; and its nature is imprecise, manifold, indirectly known. We wouldn't know it but for the element of statement present—in this case, the rumble of the Falls. But the statement is necessarily fragmentary; the principle of omission, which is what the spray served when it cancelled the visual component of the presentation, is central. Without suppression there can be no suggestion—you realize this almost at once, for the spray has subsided as abruptly as it had risen, and through a wide parting in the trees the Victoria Falls reveal their entire architecture of rock and torrent, every detail of shape, colour and movement lucid in the late August sun. This is impressive too, but in a different way.

Not only the phenomenon of the Victoria Falls with their curtain of spray, but the very name—*Musi-o-tunya*—reproduces the anatomy of suggestion. Metaphor is one of the prime movers of suggestion; the two metaphors for the spray and the sound, making up the whole name, eloquently render this truth. And the coupling of thunder and smoke (strangely reminiscent, across cultures and maybe centuries, of Mallarmé's *tonnerre et rubis*) exemplifies, generally, the output of unspoken meaning when discordant images are forcibly drawn together, and specifically, the action of that powerful lever of suggestion, synaesthesia.

The Victoria Falls are as good a case as any of nature imitating art. But poetic suggestion is indeed so many things at once or by turns that not even the Victoria Falls, for all their variety and complexity, will do as a model. Even to form a first rough idea of suggestion, we have to get away from the waterfall metaphor for poetry to poetry itself. To start with the aspect we have already looked at, suggestion can be, for one thing, suppression, resulting in truncated representation or fragmentary syntax:

> But once upon a time
> the oakleaves and the wild boars
> Antonio Antonio
> the old wound is bleeding.
> > (Herbert Read, 'Cranach')

Suggestion can be—to mention another of its many shapes and the one that is most suspect today—incantation, the eloquence of sounds and rhythms:

> For the stars and the winds are unto her
> As raiment, as songs of the harp-player;
> For the risen stars and the fallen cling to her,
> > And the southwest-wind and the west-wind sing.
> > (Swinburne, *Atalanta in Calydon*)

Or instead of the sound values of words, their opulent semantic associations can be exploited with a view to suggestiveness:

> A grief ago,
> She who was who I hold, the fats and flower,
> Or, water-lammed, from the scythe-sided thorn,
> Hell wind and sea,
> A stem cementing, wrestled up the tower,
> Rose maid and male,
> Or, masted venus, through the paddler's bowl
> Sailed up the sun.
> > (Dylan Thomas, 'A grief ago')

Suggestion can also work by realizing the alternative meanings, as distinct from the multiple associations, of words,

such as 'mede', 'peynted' and 'proces' in the following
stanza from *Troilus and Criseyde*:

> What? is this al the Ioye and al the feste?
> Is this your reed, is this my blisful cas?
> Is this the verray mede of your beheste?
> Is al this peynted proces seyd, allas!
> Right for this fyn? O lady myn, Pallas!
> Thou in this dredful cas for me purveye;
> For so astonied am I that I deye!
>
> (Chaucer)

But suggestion can equally properly be the activation of one
unspoken meaning instead of several:

> No motion has she now, no force;
>   She neither hears nor sees;
> Rolled round in earth's diurnal course,
>   With rocks, and stones, and trees.
>   (Wordsworth, 'A slumber did my spirit seal')

The unspoken meaning can often be a mood, and suggestion
then would consist in evoking the emotion through its correlative sensuous details:

> And from the first grey wakening we have found
> No refuge from the skirmishing fine rain
> And the wind that made the bell-tents heave and flap
> And the taut wet guy ropes ravel out and snap.
> All day the rain has glided, wave and mist and dream,
> Drenching the gorse and heather, a gossamer stream
> Too light to move the acorns that suddenly
> Snatched from their cups by the wild southwesterly
> Pattered against the tent and our up-turned dreaming faces.
>   (Alun Lewis, 'All day it has rained')

Suggestion is, most importantly, the diffusion of manifold meaning from a symbol or a system of symbols:

> And all shall be well and
> All manner of thing shall be well
> When the tongues of flame are in-folded
> Into the crowned knot of fire
> And the fire and the rose are one.
>
> (Eliot, 'Little Gidding')

Where suggestion is not the work of imagery, it can be a function of rhythm, of rhythm pointing to a meaning—in the following case, to a sense of the spirit's release:

> From the wide window towards the granite shore
> The white sails still fly seaward, seaward flying
> Unbroken wings.
>
> (Eliot, 'Ash Wednesday')

Rhythm can sometimes be suggestive not in the sense that it suggests a particular meaning but in the sense that it is un-resolved, disturbing, outward-pointing:

> It was not the dark filling my eyes
> And mouth appalled me; not even the drip
> Of rain like blood from the one tree
> Weather-tortured. It was the dark
> Silting the veins of that sick man
> I left stranded upon the vast
> And lonely shore of his bleak bed.
>
> (R. S. Thomas, 'Evans')

To make the same point negatively, suggestion can never

issue from the kind of rhythm that ticks with a self-contained unbroken regularity:

> The glories of our blood and state,
>   are shadows, not substantial things,
> There is no armour against Fate,
>   Death lays his icy hand on Kings,
>   Scepter and Crown,
>   Must tumble down,
> And in the dust be equal made,
> With the poor crooked sithe and spade.
>
> (Shirley, 'Death the Leveller')

The only justification for this incomplete catalogue of the elements of suggestion, reading like a schoolboy's answer to the question, 'What is suggestion?', is that it could be useful as a first quick look at the concept. Any full-length examination of the concept, however, involves an initial examination of the content and status of the term, and here we come across an ironical situation. Suggestion is clearly the prevailing mode of modern poetry, and the exploration of suggested meaning is the largest single concern of present-day criticism and scholarship. One would therefore expect 'suggestion' to be one of the overworked literary terms of our times, a cliché of criticism encountered on every page. This, however, is hardly the case. The word is not even found in the many glossaries of literary terms that have appeared in recent years. With Edgar Allan Poe and the Symbolists who were engaged in a struggle to establish the case for suggestion in opposition to other values, the word was a crucial term to be used systematically, pointedly, maybe even polemically. But when the concept has met with general acceptance and ceased to be a cause, the ascendancy and currency of the term are, paradoxically, reduced.

The experience having attained universality, its name becomes generic, and the specializations that are now understandably developed are given their own names, and these become vogue words. Refinements of the concept of suggestion have thus been worked out and labelled, and their specific names—Emotive Meaning, Ambiguity, Obliquity, Irony/Paradox, Connotation, Intension, Qualitative Progression, Texture, Gesture and so forth—have tended to eclipse the generic name in prestige and popularity.

To eclipse it, yes, but not to eliminate it. Among the passages quoted earlier as specimens of suggestion are three that were selected because they have been analysed and commented upon by the inventors of new names for suggestion, and the language of their comment is significant. The lines from *Troilus and Criseyde* are examined in Empson's chapter on the second type of ambiguity. 'Ambiguity', as used by him, is clearly a substitute for 'suggestion'. And in a passage exploring the ambiguities—or more precisely, the puns—in the lines, Empson uses the word 'suggest' as many as five times:

... And rising behind that again, heard in the indignation of the phrase, is a threat that she may expose him, and *peyn*-ted and *fyn* suggest legal pains and penalties. 'To whom do they suggest these things?' the reader may ask; and there is no obvious reply. It depends how carefully the passage is supposed to be read ... It is a more crucial question how far *peynted*, in a proper setting, can suggest 'pains'; how far we ought to leave the comparatively safe ground of ambiguity to examine latent puns ... I have sometimes wondered whether Swinburne's *Dolores* gets any of its energy from the way the word Spain, suggested by the title and by various things in the course of the poem, although one is forced to wonder what the next rhyme is going to be, never appears

B

among the dozen that are paired off with *Our Lady of Pain* . . . I want to back up my 'pains' from *peynted* by calling in 'weighted' and 'fainted' and the suggestion of labour in *all that painted*.[1]

The Wordsworth passage I have quoted was offered by Cleanth Brooks as an example of 'Irony', a term he obviously intends to be a replacement for 'suggestion'. The irony in the passage, on Cleanth Brooks's showing, springs from the opposition between the image of Lucy motionless in death and the image of the earth's rotation which involves her. But mark the phraseology of his exposition of the irony:

Wordsworth . . . attempts to *suggest* something of the lover's agonized shock at the loved one's present lack of motion—of his response to her utter and horrible inertness. And how shall he *suggest* this? He chooses to *suggest* it, not by saying that she lies as quiet as marble or as a lump of clay; on the contrary, he attempts to *suggest* it by imagining her in violent motion—violent, but imposed motion . . . (Italics mine).[2]

Tillyard similarly developed 'Obliquity' as a term to be preferred to 'suggestion'. Yet in examining the rhythm of Shirley's 'Glories of our blood' stanza as a case of the absence of Obliquity, what Tillyard does say is: 'The general tone of the metre, varied though it is by the short couplet within each stanza, is that of enunciation, not of suggestion.'[3]

Clearly the new terms cannot put 'suggestion' out of business. Perhaps the older word is the better word, after all. Also, as William Righter has argued, the terms embody valuable insights but not precise explanatory concepts and are not to be taken seriously as additions to the technical vocabulary of criticism.[4] What they have accomplished, I think, is to provide 'suggestion' with an enlarged and diversified content, now lending better definition to an existing aspect, now adding a new one; and because of them we have today fuller information than before about the mechanics of suggestion.

Take, for instance, the oldest of the new terms—Emotive Meaning (or Emotive Language). It was intended, when Richards first brought it into use, as an umbrella term for the many uses of language aside from literal or true-or-false statement—as another term, in fact, for suggestiveness. It renders explicit the most significant feature of suggestion: the inter-relatedness of the suggestive and the emotive. Richards has since moved so far away from his original position as to claim that richness (or 'resourcefulness', as he calls it) of meaning is not limited to emotive uses and is—except for the very special category of mutually defining technical terms—indeed universal in language. He takes care, however, to add that ambiguity, while it exists everywhere, is in particular 'the indispensable means of most of our most important utterances—especially in Poetry and Religion'.[5] Suggestion and emotion would thus appear to have a special relevance to each other after all.

'... Any verbal nuance, however slight, which gives room for alternative reactions to the same piece of language.'[6] Here is what one would consider an excellent definition of suggestion. It happens, however, to be Empson's definition of 'Ambiguity'. His *Seven Types* is in fact the prototypal study, in English criticism, of suggested meaning in poetry—seeing suggestion not as aura or atmosphere but as the presence of several distinct possibilities of meaning. Viewed as such, suggestion is synonymous with Ambiguity and, of all the new terms we have been discussing, Empson's gave most promise of establishing itself as the word for suggested meaning. However, Ambiguity's actual achievement has only been to add a new possible facet to suggestion. Empson's fourth and seventh types represent linguistic ambiguity in a poem as an unconscious product of some psychological ambivalence in the poet—here certainly is something that could give the study of suggestion a new and exciting direction. The New Critics and others who followed Empson copied his minute inspection of the text but stigmatized any attention to the poet's personality as the 'Intentional Fallacy', so that the latter continues to be an interest of much potential value.

Tillyard's 'Obliquity'—reminiscent of 'Indirection' which is very senior, traceable in fact to Emerson and Whitman—is obviously yet another of the proprietary names for suggestion. At once the most rewarding and the most provocative part of his exposition of Obliquity is the notion that the oblique or suggested meaning should be alien, at least apparently alien, to the statement. His identification of the main indirect meaning of *Lycidas* as the Gītā's teaching, *karmaṇyevādhikāraste Māphaleṣukadācana* ('Action alone is thy province, never the fruits thereof'), is a bold act of interpretation. His claim that this piece of obliquity is properly validated despite the absence of overt support in the poem's statement makes it bolder still.[7] There is, of course, the danger that if the link between what is said and what is suggested is too slender, the understanding will not be able to move from the one to the other. But the worse danger to the poem surely is from a hypertrophied, a tediously elaborate and obvious, link—like the correspondence between Mariana's mood and the too predictable imagery in Tennyson's poem. As Wimsatt has pointed out, too many deaths in Romantic poetry take place in winter or at night and too few lovers meet except in spring or in the countryside.[8] Tillyard's work on Obliquity has added to the content of 'suggestion' the very useful idea of an optimum distance between statement and suggested meaning.

In Cleanth Brooks's use, 'Irony' seems to mean the action of the context in disrupting the dictionary meanings of words and stimulating interinanimation between them; he also uses it to mean the association of discordant or contradictory elements. In either aspect, Irony is identical with suggestion, and both aspects are equally significant, but in Cleanth Brooks's hands the latter does seem to have been the source of a new emphasis that has helped in giving suggestion its specifically modern interest. The yoking of incompatibles is nothing new and can be traced to Coleridge's criticism or, farther back, to Aristotle's, but it is the technology of modern imagery that has made it the unique secret of suggestiveness. To Cleanth Brooks, the value of juxtaposing non-congruent concepts or images is that it is an insurance against sentimentality and a guarantee of honest taking note of the complexities and contradictions in experience. Its value, however, to suggestiveness lies in the fact that the more disparate the objects you pull toward each other, the greater seems to be the semantic energy released between them. For suggestion seen thus—as the bringing together of disparates—F. W. Bateson has his own term, 'Semantic Synthesis'.

As well as being a term in logic where it means something altogether different, 'Connotation' stands for whatever a word conveys other than its primary or dictionary meaning —other than, that is, its Denotation. This is how it is in general use; in criticism, it can refer to musical evocations, deposits of racial memory, traditional associations within or across cultures, private associations, colloquial overtones, implied ideas, affective colouring—in criticism, in short, 'Connotation' has acquired interchangeability with 'suggestion'. The value of the word lies in the very important proviso contained in the prefix *con-*. 'Con-' is 'together with'; suggested meaning is what a piece of language carries *together with* (never without) its stated meaning—there can be no connotation without denotation. Those who would abolish discourse and attempt a rarefied language where the logical meaning of words is suspended and words are purely musical notes or magic devices or pieces of string must heed the voice of the little Latin morpheme, 'con-'. Its message is, to borrow T. S. Eliot's words, ' . . . You cannot have the aura alone.'[9] Yvor Winters's—or Kenneth Burke's—term 'Qualitative Progression', which is used pejoratively, refers to the kind of suggestiveness which offers a series of images that may have internal coherence but are not buttressed by a structure of narration.

'Connotation' and 'Intension' mean roughly the same in logic, and Allen Tate's adoption of 'Intension' as a substitute for 'suggestion' looks like a case of this near-synonymity getting duplicated in criticism—although the explanation for his being attracted to the word lies less perhaps in logic than in metaphysics. Bergson's 'Intensive Manifold', which, because of Hulme, has been a seminal concept in modern criticism, has to do with intuition, unanalysable wholeness and imperviousness to paraphrase, and although Tate's own method of exploring 'intensive meaning' is verbal analysis, I think his notion of 'Intension' (which is part of a theory of 'tension') preserves, more than vestigially, the anti-intellectual orientation of Bergson's concept. The service that Tate's term does to criticism is to bring into focus the basically extra-logical character of suggestion.

John Crowe Ransom's term 'texture' denotes a poem's concrete sensuous features—the sound values, the imagery, the connotations of its language—which establish its poetic non-prosaic identity. This is, as he sees it, one component of the poem, the other being the paraphrasable statement in it which he calls 'logical structure'. This seems to be the old statement-suggestion antithesis in a different wrapping, and in so far as it is possible to discern any concepts through Ransom's somewhat opaque exposition, it does seem likely that 'texture' represents a struggle to find a more precise and expressive word for suggestion. The principal gain from Ransom's restatement is the pointing up of 'concreteness' in the suggestors as vital to a poem *per se*.

It is not easy to see quite what Blackmur means by 'Gesture', chiefly because the language in which he expounds the meaning of the term shares some of that tendency to advance beyond the literal which he regards as the differentia of language as gesture. The examples are even less helpful than the explanations. There are, however, one or two revealing asides: ' . . . that play of meaningfulness among words which cannot be defined in the formulas in the dictionary, but which is defined in their use together'[10]; ' . . . the revelation of the *sum* or *product* of all the meanings possible within the focus of the words played upon . . .'[11] It is difficult to resist the feeling that 'Gesture' so conceived is suggestion in a new suit. A valuable insight that Blackmur's essay contributes to the theory of suggestion concerns the difference between Gesture and symbol. 'Gestures are the first steps toward the making of symbols, and those symbols which endure are the residuary legatees of the meanings earned through gesture.'[12] The distinction between a symbol accomplished and a quantity of suggested meaning that is yet to develop permanence or recurrence and graduate to the status of symbol—the distinction, in other words, between suggestion as being and suggestion as becoming—can be an important one, enabling us to see suggestion as a two-stage process.

Profiting by competition with younger and more prestigious rivals, 'suggestion' seems to have drawn varied sustenance from them and gained more definition and improved differentiation. But enrichment has come to the word in another way too—not at the expense of new equivalents competing with it, but by being itself adopted as the English equivalent of an ancient Sanskrit term. The first Indologist to translate *dhvani* as 'suggestion' must have done so not because he was concerned to establish parallels between a ninth-century Indian critical tradition and a nineteenth-century Western one but merely because it seemed to be the obvious equivalent in English for *dhvani* or *vyañjanā*. The literal meaning of *dhvani* is 'sound'. (It is interesting that the concept of suggestion is expressed in English at times by means of sonic terms like resonance, reverberation, overtones and undertones.) *Dhvani* was originally a term in linguistics where it referred to the final sound in a word, which, when apprehended, suggested or revealed the phonological identity of the whole word. Borrowing the word and making it stand for the suggestion of meaning, Sanskrit semasiology and poetics had evolved, by about the middle of the ninth century, a theory of poetic meaning constructed round the notion that suggestion is a distinct function of language and indeed the principle of the highest kind of poetry, and had offered, in Ānandavardhana's *Dhvanyāloka*, a complete formulation of the theory. The theory grew out of a body of poetry very different from the output of nineteenth-century romanticism, and the modern European languages in which this movement flowered are a far cry from Sanskrit; also, the methodology of Ānandavardhana and his successors, which was ruled largely by deduction, definition and classification, has little in common with the *modus operandi* of the Symbolist critics or even of the more cerebral New Critics. Even if these divergences were not there, one would still regard analogies assumed between cultures remote from each other as fancied or superficial. Nevertheless, it is clear that in a very real sense the exponents of *dhvani* and the exponents of suggestion have been looking at the same phenomena and reaching the same findings—such as, the importance in poetry of what is not stated, the many-levelledness of poetic meaning, the alogical nature of all apprehension of unstated meaning in poetry, and objectification as the only mode of presenting emotion in poetry. The affinities ring so true that it is impossible for anyone aware of both systems to use the word 'suggestion' without thinking of all that *dhvani* denotes. The fertilization of suggestion with notions from Sanskrit is a real enough event—probably the most significant thing that has happened to the concept since the Symbolists provided Poe's airy-fairy formulation with enough conceptual meat. If this accession of meaning to 'suggestion' from Sanskrit thought has not been influential, it is only because the available expositions in English of the *dhvani* theory have either not been sufficiently comprehensible or have failed to reach more than a small circle of readers in the West.

The status of 'suggestion' is bound up with that of its opposite, 'statement', which has a shorter history—Poe preferred the phrase 'the upper current of meaning' and Mallarmé preferred *nommer* and *description*. The growth of 'statement' as a critical term has been since the turn of the century. More recently, it has had to work in competition with 'discourse', 'narration', 'argument', 'extension', 'denotation', 'Rational Progression' and other near-equivalents. 'Statement' and 'suggestion' have, however, persisted as a pair of antonyms with more serviceability and authority than any other. And unlike 'statement' which denotes what is more the exception than the rule in contemporary poetry, 'suggestion' has been acquiring greater precision as well as greater range as a generic naming device and developing extensive descriptive and evaluative uses. And, whether named as such or not, the notion itself, favoured by an aesthetic which makes the rejection of verbal explicitness the very condition of artistic expression, is now established as a key concept and as a versatile means of analysis and interpretation and is constantly adding to its refinements and diversifying and enlarging its uses.

2

Suggestion: From Poe to the Present

The first observed use of the word 'suggest' in what seems to come closest to its present sense in criticism is in Dryden's sentence (1697), 'Virgil . . . loves to suggest a truth indirectly'.[1] Another early occurrence is in Lord Kames's *Elements of Criticism* (1785): ' . . . and by suggesting various meanings at once, it [viz. "a vague or obscure expression"] is admired by others as concise and comprehensive'.[2] Dryden and Kames clearly are using the word here in its popular sense (viz. 'suggestion' as the opposite of 'direct expression') while making a critical statement. Which is, of course, very different from using it as a critical term, as for instance David Perkins does today when he says: 'No more than other romantic writers does Wordsworth spend much time speculating how the process of suggestion actually works.'[3]

In any case, the golden age of English statement poetry, to which Dryden and Kames belonged, can hardly be expected to have witnessed the hypostatization of suggestion. A more likely season for this would be the nineteenth century in England and Europe. Yet 'suggestion', as far as I am aware, does not occur as a technical word anywhere in Romantic criticism. In *On the Constitution of Church and State According to the Idea of Each*, Coleridge does speak of 'ideas which may indeed be suggested and awakened, but cannot, like the

17

images of sense and the conceptions of the understanding, be adequately expressed by words'. But the coupling of 'suggested' with 'awakened' shows that 'suggested' is not a technical word here any more than 'awakened' can be, and that Coleridge is merely using the word here like Dryden and Kames in its popular sense as the opposite of 'directly expressed'. Nor is the word, as far as I am aware, used in a technical sense in Goethe, Schiller, Schelling, the Schlegels and the other German Romantic critics. Indeed, Edgar Allan Poe, while crediting the German critics with the concept of a suggestive under-current of meaning in poetry, points out that their word for poetry with this under-current is 'mystic'.

Another area where one may hope to locate the origin of 'suggestion' as a technical term is American criticism. Although early American culture—both the commercial practicality of its material aspect and the austere Puritan plainness and logicality implicit in its spiritual aspect—was firmly wedded to the concept of language as unambiguous rational discourse, yet basically the New England imagination was allegorical or even—however incipiently—symbolistic, and we find Cotton Mather, a younger contemporary of Dryden, moving so far away from his earlier commitment to univocal simplicity as to approve of allusiveness and implication. In the eighth chapter of *Manuductio ad Ministerium* (1726), he commends the style where 'the paragraph is embellished with *profitable references*, even to something beyond what is *directly spoken*. Formal and painful quotations are not studied, yet all that could be learnt from them is insinuated.'[4] This comes pretty close to suggestion, but Mather nowhere uses the term, nor do any of the other American rhetoricians and critics who preceded Poe.

A few scattered instances of the use of 'suggest' and 'suggestive' can indeed be met with in critical writings from Dryden onwards, but clearly in none of these cases is the word used as a critical term. When does a popular word become a technical term? Of course, purely formal devices like italics, quotation marks or an initial capital letter can signal the intention that the word is technical, but in substance a word is raised above the lay lexis and established as a technical term when an element in its original popular meaning is selected and fixed by explicit definition and conscious and consistent specialized use. By this token, it is, I think, in Poe's critical writings that 'suggestiveness' is first used as a technical term.

During the years 1840–46 the nature of the imagination and of suggestion seems to have engaged Poe's attention a great deal. In his review of Thomas Moore's poem *Alciphron*, Poe rejects Coleridge's famous definition of Imagination and Fancy and sets up his own. Poems 'which mankind have been accustomed to designate as *imaginative*' are remarkable, he says, for their '*suggestive* character', by which is meant that 'there lies beneath the transparent upper current of meaning an under or *suggestive* one'. This 'mystic or secondary expression' of sentiment 'has the vast force of an accompaniment in music'. 'With each note of the lyre is heard a ghostly, and not always a distinct, but an august and soul-exalting *echo* . . . But not so in poems which the world has always persisted in terming *fanciful*. Here the upper current is often exceedingly brilliant and beautiful; but then men *feel* that this upper current is *all*.'

This is a clear enough formulation (although the terminology makes it sound somewhat inchoate) of the distinction between suggestive poetry and statement poetry.

But what is significant here is that in Poe's use the terms 'suggestive' and 'imaginative' are so intimately related as to be interchangeable. To find out the nature of the connection, we have to turn to *The Poetic Principle*. Here he defines the end of poetry as 'the Rhythmical Creation of Beauty'— beauty 'that appertains to eternity alone'—by means of the imagination; and he implies that the imagination works through 'multiform combinations among the things and thoughts of Time'. 'It is in Music, perhaps', he goes on in the same essay, 'that the soul most nearly attains the great end for which, when inspired by the Poetic Sentiment, it struggles—the creation of supernal Beauty ... And thus there can be little doubt that in the union of Poetry with Music in its popular sense, we shall find the widest field for the Poetic development.' What makes music the vehicle *par excellence* of the sense of Ideal Beauty? Poe had provided the answer several years earlier as a young man of twenty-two in the 'Letter to B——' (published as a preface in his *Poems*, 1831), where he spoke of poetry 'presenting perceptible images ... with *in*definite sensations, to which end music is an *essential*, since the comprehension of sweet sound is our most indefinite conception'. Indefiniteness is essentially suggestive. It is then by indeterminateness of expression (a quality that music possesses in a pre-eminent degree) that in poetry the imagination suggests 'Beauty'. This assumption explains why what is imaginative is invariably suggestive and why poetry is most itself when it shares the nature of music. The assumption is elaborated in *Marginalia* (XVI, 29):

... a suggestive indefinitiveness of meaning, with the view of bringing about a definitiveness of vague and therefore of spiritual *effect* ... I *know* that indefinitiveness is an element of the true music—I mean of the true musical expression. Give to it any

undue decision—imbue it with any very determinate tone—and
you deprive it, at once, of its ethereal, its ideal, its intrinsic and
essential character. You dispel its luxury of dream. You dissolve
the atmosphere of the mystic upon which it floats. You exhaust
it of its breath of faery. It now becomes a tangible and easily
appreciable idea—a thing of the earth, earthy.

This explains why Poe, while he always uses the term
'suggestive' with a precise meaning, also uses it inclusively,
equating it with 'imaginative' and often with 'mystical',
'ideal', 'beautiful', 'ethereal', 'spiritual', 'elevating', 'august'
and 'pure'.

The concept of suggestiveness, stated in such very general
terms, looks fairly convincing. But when Poe comes down
to brass tacks, the effect is anticlimactic. The poems he
enumerates as remarkable for their suggestiveness—*Prometheus Vinctus*, *The Inferno*, *The Ancient Mariner*, *Christabel*,
Kubla Khan, *The Nightingale Ode*, *The Sensitive Plant*, etc.—
are perhaps suggestive in varying degrees, but they certainly
do not isolate the differentia of suggestive writing. Poe
calls our attention to 'the *suggestive* force which exalts and
etherealizes' the passages he quotes from *Alciphron*, but anyone who looked for such force in the lines would be looking
in vain. Nor would many readily join Poe in rating Tennyson 'the noblest of poets' for suggestiveness.

The metaphors Poe employs to expound suggestiveness
—'a ghostly and not always a distinct . . . echo'; 'long and
wild vistas'; 'dim bewildering visions'—seem to point to
the symbol's freedom from equivalence to a concept and its
capacity for resonant multiple meaning. Yet in Poe's exposition of his own poem 'The Raven', it turns out that the
'under-current, however indefinite, of meaning' from which
springs the suggestiveness of the last two stanzas is, after all,

merely the idea of 'mournful and never-ending remembrance' which the bird stands for. Similarly (although we do not have Poe's word for it) the palace in 'The Haunted Palace' can stand for a deranged mind, and 'the spectre of a planet' in 'Ulalume' can stand for the semblance of love. But this is a paradox that plagued French Symbolism as well. It in fact inheres in the art of suggestion—a poet who knows that he is being suggestive cannot help suggesting *something*; a consciously used symbol inevitably develops reference. But Poe shows a way out of the dilemma. In his review of Hawthorne's *Twice-Told Tales* and *Mosses from an Old Manse*, it turns out that by 'the suggested meaning' Poe means the allegory, but it is the allegory 'seen only as a shadow or by suggestive glimpses'. The thing symbolized should never be evident or explicit. He seems to make the same point in *The Philosophy of Composition*: 'It is the *excess* of the suggested meaning—it is the rendering this the upper instead of the under current of the theme—which turns into prose (and that of the very flattest kind) the so called poetry of the so called transcendentalists.'

Poe's concept of indefiniteness is very suspect today—we have moved away from it and all the way along the scale to Hulme's concept of 'accurate, precise and definite description'. Also, the words Poe uses as near-synonyms of 'suggestive'—words like 'ideal', 'ethereal', 'elevating', 'august', and 'pure'—will offend present-day taste. In fact Poe's whole formulation of the principle of suggestiveness is in terms that tend to validate second-rate Romantic poetry.

But it was Poe's broad theoretical formulation broadly apprehended, and not at all either his specific applications of it or his own poetic practice, that made 'suggestion' a key term in subsequent criticism. The consistent and self-conscious, if a little immature and ebullient, use of the word 'suggestive' in Poe's incidental theorizing in successive essays and reviews had the effect of establishing it as a technical term in criticism. It was transmitted from Poe to his younger contemporaries and successors in American criticism. Henry Timrod's essay, *Theory of Poetry* (1863), which is largely a defence of the long poem against Poe's attack, reaffirms nevertheless Poe's principle of suggestion and does so in language very similar to Poe's:

. . . and the poetry of words has never so strange a fascination as when it seems to suggest more than it utters, to call up by implication rather than by expression those thoughts which refuse to be embodied in language, and to hint at something ineffable and mysterious of which the mind can attain but partial glimpses.[5]

Both Emerson and Whitman use 'indirections' as an alternative term to 'suggestion'. Whitman, however, uses the term 'suggestion' at least twice. In 'Democratic Vistas' he mentions how the poet 'seldomer tells a thing than suggests or necessitates it'. In 'A Backward Glance O'er Travel'd Roads' (1888), the preface to the ninth and last edition of *Leaves of Grass*, he names the distinctive quality of the *Leaves*: 'The word I myself put primarily for the description of them as they stand at last is the word Suggestiveness.'

It was French criticism, not American, that seriously took over the concept of suggestiveness, developing full-bloodedly the various significations it had acquired in Poe's handling of it and erecting a poetic round it. Poe's triple sway over nineteenth-century French literature—as man, as poet and

C

as critic—is one of the strangest episodes of literary history. Baudelaire, Mallarmé and Valéry, although they essentially formed a single tradition, received Poe's influence independently of each other and through an imperfectly learnt English language. J. Isaacs felt that in particular Poe's influence on their criticism—specifically, in regard to the notion that poetry partakes of the nature of music—was uncanny, as none of them, he was sure, could have read Poe's review of *Alciphron* where this notion is offered.[6] But it is also offered, as our quotations above show, in his other critical writings which were accessible enough to his French admirers, and there is no need to suspect clairvoyance.

The French Symbolists' theoretical pronouncements seem themselves to exemplify some of the virtues—indirection, vagueness, obscurity—that they celebrate as the soul of poetry, so that in making a summary in order to show how the concept of suggestion can be claimed to have generated the tenets of Symbolism, it is necessary to reduce everything to points even if that tends to make things appear clearer and simpler than such things ever could be.

1. Objects in the phenomenal universe

(*a*) suggest the supra-sensible reality beyond them, and

(*b*) suggest one another across the barriers between the arts and across the barriers between the senses. ('*Ce qui serait vraiment surprenant, c'est que le son ne pût suggérer la couleur, que les couleurs ne pussent pas donner l'idée d'une mélodie, et que le son et la couleur fussent impropres à traduire les idées.*' Baudelaire)

2. The poet uses these objects

(*a*) to suggest macrocosm (i.e., transcendental reality/ the Idea/the Essence), or

(*b*) to suggest microcosm (i.e., a state of mind, an

emotion). ('... *choisir un objet et en dégager un état d'âme, par une série de déchiffrements.*' Mallarmé)
Neither of these would admit of being presented otherwise than by suggestion.

3. The poet presents the object itself not by naming or description but by suggestion (i.e., allusion, gradual evocation). ('*Nommer un objet, c'est supprimer les trois quarts de la jouissance du poème qui est faite de deviner peu à peu: le suggérer, voilà le rêve. C'est le parfait usage de ce mystère qui constitue le symbole: évoquer petit à petit un objet ...*' Mallarmé)

4. The poet's word instead of representing the sensuous exterior of the object (the palpable trees) suggests the essence, the atmosphere (the forest's shudder).

5. The poet abolishes the word's meaning (= logical meaning) and liberates suggestion (= associations) from its sound.

6. Music is the suggestive art *par excellence*, performing all the functions listed above better than any other art. Poetry should strive to approximate to music. ('*Et pour suggérer les émotions ... un signe special a été inventé: le son musical.*' Wyzéwa)

7. Indefiniteness/mystery/obscurity as elements of suggestiveness. ('... *quelque chose d'un peu vague, laissant carrière à la conjecture ... Le mystère, le regret sont aussi des caractères du Beau.*' Baudelaire)

These jottings will serve to show how suggestion, explicitly so called, is central to the Symbolist aesthetic; it would be strange if it were not, for the symbol is after all a suggestive device. It will also be clear that the main features of this carefully wrought aesthetic can be traced to the insights that Poe expressed so fumblingly and superficially in his theorizings on suggestion: Ideal Beauty;

indefiniteness; poetry sharing the nature of music; and (although I have not touched upon these) suggestiveness implying short-flightedness and the-poem-for-its-own-sake. The noblest tribute Poe has earned so far from anywhere comes from that doyen of Australian literature, A. D. Hope: 'There would be no point in contemplating the ingenious but essentially trivial arguments of Poe's *The Poetic Principle* had these arguments not had the misfortune to justify so aptly what was going on in poetic practice in the nineteenth century, and had they not, by a series of unfortunate accidents, become the basis of so many varieties of modern poetic doctrine.'[7] The biggest of these unfortunate accidents is, of course, the Symbolist Movement.

Any survey of the history of suggestion in our own century is complicated by the paradox (mentioned in the last chapter) that while the phenomenon has become universal in literature and interest in it has become universal in criticism, the term itself has limited currency, so that the historian has to restrict his range to suggestion-named-as-such. This is a large enough area though, and within it the concept, while preserving a recognizable continuity from Poe to Perkins, has moved along new lines of development.

At the turn of the century, A. C. Bradley, in his Oxford Inaugural, *Poetry for Poetry's Sake* (1901), described suggestion as a case of the poem pointing beyond itself to an all-embracing perfection which can only be partially manifested through language; by a mysterious resonance, what is stated expands into an infinity of suggestion.[8] Bradley was the first heir to the spiritual-transcendental conception of suggestion that the Symbolists worked on; he was probably also the last, as attention was soon to shift from the magical to the semantic aspect of suggestion. In philosophy, in linguistics, in literary criticism, the new century was one that was destined to become a uniquely semasiological era. Already, a year before Bradley's Inaugural, Yeats in the essay *The Symbolism of Poetry* (1900) had spoken of 'innumerable meanings, which are held to "white" or to "purple" by bonds of subtle suggestion'.[9] This is not to say that interest in suggestion as a mystique died out altogether. In his *Phases of English Poetry*, Sir Herbert Read is found saying: 'Suggestion, in my opinion, covers all those vague notions which the Abbé Bremond has wrapped in fluffy phrases, such as "mystery", "enchantment", "intimate nature of the soul", "magic" and so on.'[10] This was in 1928, but about this time suggestion was already parting company with vagueness and fluffiness.

The transition from suggestion-as-magic to suggestion-as-meaning is vividly demonstrated in Lascelles Abercrombie's critical ambivalence. He could speak of 'verbal magic' and 'the enchantment of language'[11] but he also defines suggestion as the business of liberating the secondary meanings —intensities and complexities of sense—that cluster round the word's dictionary definition, in order to render the 'sensuous impressions, psychological intuitions and the mass of infinitely variable associations' that, along with the thought element they surround, compose the experience the poet is trying to express.[12]

One of the earliest to question the Symbolist assumption that meaning and suggestion are opposed principles was, interestingly enough, a distinguished heir to Symbolism: T. S. Eliot. In the essays on Marvell and Dryden (1921) he notes how in Morris's poetry (or at least in the lines he examines) and in Swinburne's, suggestion is abortive because statement is absent—their language is all connotation and no denotation.[13] By replacing suggestion-versus-meaning with the antithesis connotation-versus-denotation, Eliot equates suggestion with connotational meaning. The demolition of the theory of suggestion as non-meaning was completed by F. W. Bateson in his *English Poetry: a Critical Introduction* (1950) with the dictum, 'A word's connotation is as much a part of its meaning as its denotation'.[14] Four years later, in *The Verbal Icon*, W. K. Wimsatt was even claiming that 'suggestion' was a better word than 'connotation' for this department of meaning; the suggestion/statement antithesis, he felt, was simpler and clearer, as connotation/denotation and intension/extension have a different technical sense in logic and can thus be misleading.[15] A more recent description of suggestion (by John Bayley in *The Romantic Survival*, 1957) as 'casting the net of reference in a wider and more subjective arc'[16] shows that the process of redefining suggestion as a branch of meaning is now complete.

Parallel to this growing attention to suggestion as meaning there has been the development of interest in suggestion as an event in the reader's consciousness. Defining suggestion negatively in terms of the Parnassians' method, Mallarmé had said of them: '. . . *ils retirent aux esprits cette joie délicieuse de croire qu'ils créent.*' And in the passage on suggestiveness (which I quoted from) in Whitman's preface to his *Leaves of Grass*, he further says:

I round and finish little, if anything; and could not, consistently with my scheme. The reader will always have his or her part to do, just as much as I have had mine. I seek less to state or display any theme or thought, and more to bring you, reader, into the atmosphere of the theme or thought—there to pursue your own flight.

This approach to suggestion, which regards suggested meaning as a construct of the reader's mind, has had greater appeal for some than suggestion as the harvest of the text. In *Poetic Diction* (1928), Owen Barfield makes the point that meaning essentially is intuited by the listener or reader and that suggestion is the play of 'poetic imaginative sympathy' which makes such intuition possible.[17] The theory of suggestion as reader-participation has been an abiding interest at Harvard. W. J. Bate understands by suggestion the way poetry, through indefiniteness or incompleteness, rouses the reader's imagination to creative activity.[18] His student, David Perkins, in his *Wordsworth and the Poetry of Sincerity* (1964), refers to the notion of suggestion as 'the calling up of what is already there in the reader's mind', only to point out that this is not what happens when we read *The Prelude*. When mystic experience such as Wordsworth's, to which the reader's own life has no parallels, has to be communicated, suggestion operates by getting the reader's mind to 'work creatively upon the poem', so that the reader 'goes beyond what can be said in words, himself leaping the gap and arriving at the intuition in the poet's mind'.[19] The reader's collaboration is, in fact, what distinguishes suggestion in literature from suggestion in cinema. In an *Encounter* article which appeared some eight years ago, Nicola Chiaromonte makes the point that the non-verbal suggestive effect of the cinematographic image is immediate and deterministic while the response to the suggestiveness of language calls for the mind's active intervention: 'The cinema derives its power from its ability to arouse an emotional reaction that is both immediate and certain. Whereas a poem or a novel cannot come alive without the reader's elaboration; its power of suggestion is a construction of his mind, calling into play his sensibility, and his intellectual and imaginative faculties.'

Exciting as it can be, speculation is all that is possible about what happens in a mind exposed to suggestion. Certainly, the more worthwhile of the two lines of development that the concept has followed is the one that has obeyed the trend in modern taste and criticism and led to the identification of suggestion with unstated interpretable layers of meaning. It is this aspect of it that has absorbed the additions and refinements offered by Ambiguity, Irony and other novel formulations and acquired a depth, reach and precision that could more than make up for its not being a vogue word.

3

Suggestion through the Objective Correlative

If people do not talk about the 'objective correlative' any more, it is not because it has been found untenable and furtively dropped. Rather it has ceased to be debatable—its axiomatic status has now been conceded. The criticisms brought up when T. S. Eliot enunciated it in 1919 were that the phrase was ugly and the idea one of strictly local validity at best, that it applied only to dramatic poetry, that it really applied only to Eliot's work, that it applied only to *Hamlet*, that it did not apply even to *Hamlet*. Eliot now faces objections which are the very opposite of these—that the idea is nothing new and that even the phrase (which thirty-eight years after he first used it Eliot was still feeling pleased with himself for having coined)[1] is not Eliot's but one Washington Allston's.[2] (Credit for 'dissociation of sensibility' has similarly been transferred by Mr Bateson to Rémy de Gourmont.[3]) But if Eliot is to have no share of the honours, the universality of the objective correlative has nevertheless now been accepted to the extent that the most influential criticism of our times is concerned with the intensive study of the correlates of emotion—imagery, sound values, and to a lesser extent, plot and character—within the verbal organization where they occur and belong.

Eliot's critics are right—the objective correlative was neither invented nor discovered by Eliot. Indeed its value lies precisely in the fact that it was not invented or discovered by him. It is as old as poetry itself. If the impression has gained ground that Eliot in his criticism erected the objective correlative as a principle and kept talking about it while he was writing the kind of poetry which works by objectification of feeling through dramatic detail and that his criticism put the objective correlative aside when his poetry did not need it any more, he has largely himself to blame. In 1942 in his Ker Memorial lecture on *The Music of Poetry*, Eliot the elderly arbiter of taste went out of his way to cast doubt on the *bona fides* of Eliot the young critic. As a critic, the poet, he said, 'at the back of his mind, if not as his ostensible purpose, is always trying to defend the kind of poetry he is writing, or to formulate the kind that he wants to write'. This is the case, Eliot warned his audience, 'especially when he is young, and actively engaged in battling for the kind of poetry which he practises'.[4] Eliot, the young poet-critic of the 'twenties, by claiming for the method of myth and image the status of a discovery, had given the impression of setting up a theoretical formulation which would be an oblique apology for his poetry. When *Ulysses* appeared, he hailed its use of 'the mythical method'—the rendering of emotion or inward experience through direct sensuous embodiment in concrete image—as a revolution. It was less a revolution than a correction of the tendency to discursiveness that had been steadily growing as the mythopoeic faculty, after Keats and Shelley, weakened. But the various guides to T. S. Eliot took the cue from his manifesto for the mythical method and proceeded to show industriously how each poem of Eliot's was an old curiosity shop of objective correlatives, from Mr Appollinax's head rolling under a chair or grinning over a screen right down to the twisted shape at the first turning of the second stair in *Ash Wednesday*. Here the guides paused, for *Four Quartets* had signally fewer of these oddments to offer. It was then assumed that Eliot had passed from dramatic objectification to direct poetic philosophizing. And so he had, but only fitfully, and as large parts of the *Quartets* show, the dramatic externals, the sensory correlates were never really dispensed with. As B asks in *A Dialogue on Dramatic Poetry*, what great poetry is not dramatic?[5]

The objective correlative as formulated by Eliot—palpable, precise, clear—was sired by the Imagist image. Hulme's orthodox doctrine, of course, regarded the dry, hard, specific 'thing' as self-sufficient, needing no emotional complement, but Pound diluted this to the extent of conceding that the natural object, while being its distinct concrete definite self, 'presents an intellectual and emotional complex'. But that, apart from the *magie* and the *mysticisme*, was what the Symbolist symbol was already doing. Mallarmé's *salle d'ébène* or his *pourpre la roue du seul vespéral de mes chars* is the external correlate of an otherwise ineffable *état d'âme*.

Objects as suggestive associates of emotion are necessarily present in all poetry, although one period, type or form may need them more than the others do or use them differently. It may be said—but only as a very general principle—that in art, states of sentience are expressed through their sensuous equivalents. As Wimsatt and Beardsley put it in their essay, 'The Affective Fallacy', emotions in poetry are 'not communicated to the reader like an infection or disease, not inflicted mechanically like a bullet or knife wound, not administered like a poison, not simply expressed as by expletives, grimaces or rhythms, but presented in their objects and contemplated as a pattern of knowledge'.[6]

The *locus classicus* on the objective correlative is the latter half of Eliot's essay on *Hamlet:*

Mr. Robertson is undoubtedly correct in concluding that the essential emotion of the play is the feeling of a son towards a guilty mother . . . The only way of expressing emotion in the form of art is by finding an 'objective correlative'; in other words, a set of objects, a situation, a chain of events which shall be the formula of that *particular* emotion; such that when the external facts, which must terminate in sensory experience, are given, the emotion is immediately evoked . . . The artistic 'inevitability' lies in this complete adequacy of the external to the emotion; and this is precisely what is deficient in *Hamlet*. Hamlet (the man) is dominated by an emotion which is inexpressible, because it is in *excess* of the facts as they appear . . . His disgust is occasioned by his mother, but . . . his mother is not an adequate equivalent for it . . . And it must be noticed that the very nature of the *données* of the problem precludes objective equivalence. To have heightened the criminality of Gertrude would have been to provide the formula for a totally different emotion in Hamlet; it is just *because* her character is so negative and insignificant that she arouses in Hamlet the feeling which she is incapable of representing.[7]

This could be Ānandavardhana in the ninth century judging a play or a poem in terms of the theory of *Rasa-dhvani* (the Suggestion of Emotion) of which he was the first exponent. Eliot's concepts and terms here are uncannily similar to those of Sanskrit criticism. The 'essential emotion' is the dominant *rasa*. Disgust is *jugupsā*, one of the eight *sthāyins* (permanent emotions). Gertrude is the human object of the emotion—the *ālambanavibhāva*. The inadequacy of

objective equivalence that Eliot complains of would have
been called a *rasa-doṣa* (a flaw in the presentation of emotion)
by Mammaṭa (11th–12th century) and an *anaucitya* (a case of
inappropriateness) by Kṣemendra (11th century). The only
difference (though it is an important difference) is that the
Sanskrit terms denote a failure on the dramatist's part, while
Eliot's point is that the inadequacy in objectification inheres
in the situation in the play.

The cardinal concept of Indian aesthetics is *rasa*. *Rasa*
literally means tincture, taste, flavour, relish. It has been
variously translated as 'Sentiment', 'Aesthetic Emotion',
Stimmung, Geschmack, Saveur. But all these words have other
connotations which can mislead and confuse. What then is
rasa? There is the well-known enunciation by Viśvanātha
(14th century):

Rasa, experienced by men of sensibility, is born of the dominance
of the *sattva* principle, is indivisible, self-manifested, compounded
of joy and consciousness, untouched by aught else perceived,
brother to the realization of *brahman*, and its very life is unearthly
wonder.

This is so loftily metaphysical that one is glad to fall back
on Bharata's simple metaphor for *rasa*—the sensation on the
palate! Even more simply, *rasa* can be described as the
response to art. It has all the features of the aesthetic experience familiar to Western philosophy—it is emotion
objectified, universalized; and raised to a state where it
becomes the object of lucid disinterested contemplation and
is transfigured into serene joy . . . This is as far as a non-
philosopher can get in defining the nature of the *rasa* experience.

Rasa thus grows out of, is a consummation of, the emotion

presented in art. Ancient Indian psychology—the one, at any rate, which Abhinavagupta (10th–11th century) made use of —assumed nine heads under which all emotional activity could be grouped: the sexual emotion, amusement, distress, anger, masterfulness (energy), fear, disgust, wonder and subsidence. These are permanent emotions (*sthāyins*) sprung from universal psychic dispositions (*vāsanās*) in human nature and lie inert within a man except when a stimulus activates them for a while. (*Sthāyins* are a universal human equipment, and all men are potentially capable of the realization of *rasa*. Actually, however, only the *sahṛdaya* or *rasika*—the man of either inborn or trained sensibility— can realize *rasa*.) The nine categories are mutually exclusive and claimed to be together exhaustive, so that whichever emotion the poem or play expresses or arouses must come under one *sthāyin* or the other.

How does a poem present or convey an emotion? Sanskrit theory has an answer that is by no means unique to it: a poem does so through the objective correlatives of the emotion. Images, characters, situations which are the objec- tive correlatives of the emotion are presented descriptively in a poem and, when the reader's mind makes contact with these, they awaken the corresponding *sthāyin* within him and raise it to the state of *rasa*. Nine specific *rasa*s grow out of the nine *sthāyin*s:

Sthāyins	Rasas
Rati (the sexual emotion)	*Śṛṅgāra* (love)
Hāsa (laughter/amusement)	*Hāsya* (the comic)
Śoka (grief/distress)	*Karuṇa* (pathos)
Krodha (anger)	*Raudra* (anger)
Utsāha (masterfulness/energy)	*Vīra* (the heroic)

Bhaya (fear)	*Bhayānaka* (fear)
Jugupsā (disgust)	*Bībhatsa* (disgust)
Vismaya (wonder)	*Adbhuta* (wonder)
Śama (subsidence)	*Śānta* (serenity)

The first three acts, to take an example, of Kālidāsa's *Śakuntala* (*c.* 4th century) are an idyll that fairly teems with the objective correlatives of the *śṛṅgāra rasa*. There is Śakuntalā herself, the hermit's adopted daughter, who has lit a blaze in the King's heart. The creeper in bloom, the mango tree with its young sprouts, the bold and greedy bee, the bower on the bank of the Mālinī, the drowsy warmth of the lotus-scented air, the *uśīra* paste spread to cool the fever of Śakuntalā's breast, and many more intoxicants of the heart fill king and maid with an overmastering passion. It will not be held down either by the timidity and bashfulness of the girl or by the circumspection and dignity of the King and declares itself in tokens of word, look, gesture and action—by the fever in Śakuntalā's limbs, by the colour that rises to her cheeks, by the distraughtness and emaciation of the King. The love of Duṣyanta and Śakuntalā reaches the reader's imagination through this multitude of sensory correlates and activates a *sthāyin* that he shares with all kings and all subjects, and he is soon reliving their love less intensely but more richly and serenely.

Objective correlatives are primarily representations *in art* of the actual causes (*laukika-kāraṇas*) and the actual consequences or manifestations (*laukika-kāryas*) of an emotion *in life*. Representations of causes are called *vibhāva*s and representations of manifestations are called *anubhāva*s. The actual factors of an emotion in life are transformed thus into the conventional associates of the same emotion in art. They have a purely aesthetic existence—they are not real or practical, but idealized; they are not personal or particular, but universalized; they have no conative drift and are objects of a detached untroubled contemplation that does not issue in action. When the sensuous objects of an emotion, thus universalized in art, impinge upon an emotional set latent in the reader's consciousness, the two coalesce and give rise to the state of utter aesthetic satisfaction known as *rasa*.

But what precisely is the nature of the relationship between the sensuous correlates and the emotion—the nature of the process by which they give rise to the emotion? Bharata (*c.* 1st century), whose *Nātyaśāstra* puts forward the earliest known exposition of *rasa*, had declared laconically that a conjunction of the correlates of emotion give rise to the *rasa*. How exactly it did so he had not explained—he left that to the commentators! The first of these, Lollaṭa, offered the naturalistic version: in art, correlates produce an emotion exactly as actual causes do in life; the sorrow that fills the *Sundarakāṇḍa* of the *Rāmāyaṇa* is felt by the reader as a sorrow residing in a real Sītā. Śaṅkuka offered a logician's account: the relation of the object to the emotion is the same as that of the middle term (*sādhana*) to the major term (*sādhya*)—one, that is, of inference; the realization of *rasa* is an act of cognition, made 'relishable' by the charm of art. These explanations missed both the essential subjectivity of the *rasa* experience and the essential distinction between objects in art and objects in reality. Bhaṭṭanāyaka described the process of realizing *rasa* as comprising the universalization of experience and the elevation of the emotion (within the reader) to a state of ideal joy.

This was a valuable advance, but it left the process of *rasa*-realization still obscure.

It was given to Abhinavagupta to achieve the break-through in this controversy about what Bharata's aphorism on *rasa*-realization meant. The emotion, he said, was already there within the reader—as the *sthāyin*. The correlates therefore do not produce or generate it but only render it manifest. Emotion emerges from its descriptively presented correlates exactly as the suggested meaning (*vyaṅgyārtha*) emerges from the stated meaning—by the operation of the function of suggestion (*vyañjanā*) which is inherent in language. Emotion is suggested meaning.

When the realization of *rasa* was thus explained in terms of *dhvani* (suggestion of meaning), the whole phenomenon swung into focus. It became clear that the emotion is the image's resonance—and not reference, nor inference. Reference is denotation—a given word standing simply, precisely and invariably for a given referent. Suggested emotion, on the other hand, is in the nature of connotational meaning—complex, rich, relatively imprecise, variable. Object-emotion associations for members of the same culture are, of course, bound to have a high common factor, but they can never have the precision and universality of denotational meanings. The object of an emotion thus is not a referential sign, but an evocative symbol. Nor is the realization of the emotion a process of inference. Given the object, the emotion does not necessarily follow. The object is not bound to the emotion by a cause-and-effect relation or by invariable concomitance. The object is only the suggestive associate of the emotion.

Dhvani thus explains *rasa*; in fact the two together (*rasa-dhvani*) are the supreme mode of poetic expression. Perhaps no other case exists of one major critical tenet lighting up

D

another so much, of two independent critical traditions en-
riching each other so much and eventually coalescing. Its
affirmation that all emotion in poetry is suggested and its
version of how this is done are, I think, Sanskrit's most
valuable contribution to the theory of poetry.

From the principle that the main business of poetry is
to present emotion by suggestion, Sanskrit theory was led
naturally to the principle that every poem should have
emotional unity. Ānandavardhana insists that a poem, however long, elaborate or diversified, is ruled by a single
principal *rasa*. The *Rāmāyaṇa*, consisting of 24,000 verses,
is governed by a principal emotion. So is the *Mahābhārata*,
consisting of 100,000 verses. (That the presiding *rasa* of the
Mahābhārata—an epic that tells of the greatest war of Indian
legend—should be found to be *śānta* (serenity or quietude)
and that of the *Rāmāyaṇa*—a poem which, if the *Uttarakāṇḍa*
is not admitted to the Valmīki canon, ends with the restora-
tion of Sītā to Rāma and of Rāma to the throne—would (I
think) still be *karuṇa* (pathos) shows how the concept of *rasa*
can uncover an undercurrent of feeling which the surface life
of the poem belies.) All that happens in the poem—rhythm,
language, imagery, action, character—must be contributory to the final cumulative emotional effect. Does this
mean that the tyranny of the presiding emotion imposes on
a poem a homogeneity wholly alien to it, inhibiting the
amplitude and diversity of an art organism's life? A. B.
Keith, for instance, finds Sanskrit drama over-stylized and
wooden and puts this down to the forcible orientation of
everything in the play to a single central *rasa*.[8] But it need
not be, it indeed never is, just one emotion. The principal
rasa, itself rich, diversified and complex, is fed by a multi-
plicity of minor incidental feelings (*vyabhicārins*), and also

accommodates other *rasa*s which are subordinate to it in the poem, being developed in this or that part of it and dropped when done with. In the *Śākuntala*, love is the master motif, but there are other motifs—sorrow, tenderness, serenity, laughter. The principal emotion is thus one among many and derives its special status only from the fact that it permeates the poem, the poem indeed sums itself up in it— and also from the fact that the other emotions, while freely and fully orchestrated, are carefully harmonized with it by assimilation, by balance or by tension. If this were not so, if the poem were an essay in a single emotion, it would be unendurable. A poem is essentially a system of emotions, and the unity which the principal *rasa* establishes is a unity in diversity.

A quick *résumé* like this cannot do justice to a critical system which investigated in profuse detail the suggestion of emotions through their objects and found this to be the central business of poetry. But the summary may prove handy when we go on now to enquire whether the system which the *Dhvanyāloka* represents has any real points of contact with, or important implications for, the tradition to which Eliot's essay on *Hamlet* belongs.

The concept of nine or more *sthāyin*s or permanent emotions seems to be an oversimplification beside what we have learnt (from psychology, psycho-analysis and art) about our being's darkest and deepest region—the unconscious and the instinctual—with its minute differentiation and in-finite proliferation, and beside what the Symbolists have taught us about the uniqueness of each fugitive tone and shade of emotion. Yet psychologists and poets have in fact often tended to talk in terms of emotional stereotypes. In

the early 'twenties, William McDougall attempted an enumeration of the 'Primary Emotions' in the descending order
of specificity and distinctness, and the *sthāyin*s, all of them
but one, form the upper half of his list.[9] And a poet like
Robin Skelton can talk of poetry arousing 'love, anger,
enthusiasm, scorn, pity, hate and laughter'.[10] To try to
isolate thus the primary forms of our emotional life is not
to deny its darkness and immeasurability.

As for the doctrine of the singular nuance or instant of
emotion, it led, as we know, to a self-conscious precision of
expression, but also, in certain cases, to failure of communication. The felt urge now for rebuilding the bridges, the new
awareness of the social function and destiny of imaginative
writing, the concept of imagination as race-experience—all
these have taught us to regard what is shared as at least as
important as what is incommunicably personal. No one
today will claim for poetry that it is wholly an awakening of
universal dispositions or wholly an expression of unique
sensibility—the two run ever into each other. The exponents
of *Rasa-dhvani* insist that presentation in art individualizes a
universal emotion. The *Dhvanyāloka* explains how each time
an emotion is presented again, the process of suggestion
renders it new. The character of the emotion as it gets
expressed is uniquely determined by the 'conjunction of
correlatives'. Since no set of objects can be identical with
another, an emotion, each time it is presented, necessarily
offers a different refinement or facet of itself.

The first important concept of the *Rasa-dhvani* theory
thus is the *sthāyin*, the subjective source of *rasa*. The second
is that of the *vibhāva*s and *anubhāva*s—the objective correlatives of *rasa*. Bharata, who first formulated these, is

separated from Eliot by some twenty centuries, and if Bharata's *vibhāvas* and Eliot's 'set of objects' are placed side by side, it may be difficult to recognize them as the same articles. In subsequent theory and, of course, in poetry, the *vibhāvas* were a great deal less naïve than in Bharata's *Nātyaśāstra*, but we must nevertheless see them as they were first set forth by the Father of Sanskrit Poetics. For grief, Bharata's correlatives are the death of the loved one, loss of wealth, captivity and exile. For love ('love in union' as distinct from 'love in separation'), his correlatives are the season (spring), the loved one, the garden, garlands, unguents, ornaments. Compare these correlatives with MacLeish's:

> For all the history of grief
> An empty doorway and a maple leaf
> For love
> The leaning grasses and two lights above the sea.

('Ars Poetica')

Bharata's correlatives are the immediate sensory equivalents of the emotion—they are direct, explicit, public, conventional. MacLeish's are closer to symbols, more concentrated and potently suggestive, arbitrary and private and yet strangely eloquent, independent and free-standing, being neither naturally nor traditionally connected with the emotions they evoke. Of the symbol as such—risen from the unconscious, non-discursive, autonomous, productive of manifold meaning—Sanskrit criticism was largely innocent. (The *alaṁkāra* (trope) is, of course, a product of the imagination and, according to Ānandavardhana, is a servant to suggested emotion, and where based on metaphor, it comes pretty close to being an image, but it is at best a figure and at worst—as the name implies—an embellishment.) MacLeish's leaning grasses are a far cry from Bharata's unguents and garlands and even from Kālidāsa's richly evocative jasmine creeper and bee which, relatively sophisticated, are nevertheless firmly traditional. Yet the difference is only one of degree, and all these objects, in varying degrees, answer to Eliot's description of the objective correlative: '. . . when the external facts, which must terminate in sensory experience, are given, the emotion is immediately evoked.' Bharata's garlands are closer to the leaning grasses than to the garlands at the florist's.

Sanskrit criticism does not let us forget for a moment that the poet's garland and the florist's are two qualitatively different entities. How objects of emotion in art differ from real objects has already been touched upon, but what is the actual process that effects this transformation? Sanskrit aesthetics has the same answer as Western aesthetics: universalization. Now this is an overworked term in aesthetics and can mean either a great deal or very little. Clichés like 'de-personalization' and *sub specie eternitatis* and 'the concrete universal' are not of much help. How in Eliot's own case private images became objective correlatives with a general significance, his critics have not been able to explain. One of them thinks Eliot hit upon potentially universal images by chance;[11] Eliot himself feels that 'consciously concrete' images, if 'clearly rendered', become 'unconsciously general'.[12] This is not of much help either. A great deal of important work has, of course, been done on the growth of facts into symbols, not in the hands of an individual poet but by a slow process of evolution. A version of this process which seems to have special relevance to the theory that emotion is suggested through its objects is offered by Wimsatt and Beardsley in the essay I quoted from earlier. They point out how 'fictitious or poetic statement, where a large component of suggestion (and hence metaphor) has usually appeared' creates 'out of a mere case of factual reason for intense emotion a specified, figuratively fortified and permanent object of less intense but far richer emotion'.[13] By attaching emotion to object (horror to the murder of Duncan, or pathos to Shylock) poetry confers on both a permanence which enables them to persist through changes in culture. The historical Cleopatra is a fact, a cause in reality of Marcus Antoninus's infatuation. Shakespeare's Cleopatra is a symbol of love. The former is the actual cause of an emotion, the latter a suggestive associate of it. This is how stories grow into recurrent myths—objective universalized forms of expression for experiences that are conceived inwardly and uniquely.

Yet no account of universalization which regards it as a way of treating the material of poetry will ever be quite satisfactory. Sanskrit theory defines universalization not as a process to which the poet subjects his material but as something which goes on inside the reader's mind. According to Abhinavagupta, universalization (sādhāraṇīkaraṇa) is brought about by qualities of style, figurative expression and rhythm and (in the theatre) also by music, song and dance. These obviously affect not the poet's material but the reader's or spectator's mind which then finds itself withdrawn from reality into a world of formal beauty where the real, the personal and the particular seem to have no place and it is easy for him to realize Cleopatra within himself not as a glamorous Ptolemy of the 1st century B.C. but as a woman who loved and was loved, indeed, in a way, as all women who ever loved and were loved.

The enumeration of the traditional objective correlatives of given emotions in Sanskrit criticism would make one feel that the poet starts with an emotion to express and looks round for its external equivalents. This is, in fact, according to Graham Hough, the case against Eliot's principle. 'I wish', says Graham Hough, 'to point to . . . the suggestion that the whole natural world offers to the poet a collection of bric-à-brac from which he takes selections to represent emotional states . . . Plainly an eccentric view of the poet's procedure . . . Gerard Manley Hopkins wrote "The Wreck of the Deutschland" because he was moved by the account of a shipwreck in which five nuns were drowned; he did not go round looking for a suitable disaster to match an emotion that he already had.'[14] Raymond Williams agrees that 'Mr Eliot's statement of the matter implies an ordered process, in which the particular emotion is first understood, and an objective correlative subsequently found for it'. But (he observes) in another sense, objective correlatives 'may serve as a precipitant to the artist, in that through their comprehension the artist is able to find a provisional pattern of experience . . . Finding the objective correlative may often be for the artist the final act of evaluation of the particular experience, which will not have been completely understood until its mode of expression has been found.'[15] Whatever it be that happens at the poet's end, Sanskrit theory is quite clear that in the reader's consciousness the set of objects and the emotion arise almost, if not absolutely, simultaneously. The objective and the subjective are thus inseparable, co-extensive. The suggested meaning (the emotion) springs instantaneously from the stated meaning (the objects), the process being so rapid that its stages are imperceptible (asaṁlakṣyakrama).

The third important concept of the *Rasa-dhvani* theory

—that of a dominant emotion holding the whole poem together—is not unique to Sanskrit. 'Unity of impression', 'emotional unity', 'total response' and several other formulations, which are similar to, if not identical with, that of the dominant *rasa* are met with in Western criticism. The oldest and most prestigious of these is, of course, that of pity and fear and of tragedy through them 'effecting its katharsis of such emotions'. It is tempting to equate pity and fear with the *karuṇa* and *bhayānaka rasas*, but what Aristotle meant by emotions here is clearly different from what Ānandavardhana meant by *rasas*. Pity and fear, as seen by Aristotle, are not emotions presented in the play; they are emotions called up in the reader or spectator by what the play presents—emotions, that is, which are his reactions to the emotions presented in the play. According to the *rasa* theory, on the other hand, the emotion which the reader experiences is the same as the emotion presented in the poem—a heightened version certainly, but essentially the same emotion. The emotion presented by the poet through its objective correlates; the permanent emotion (*sthāyin*) awakened in the reader; the *rasa* he finally experiences—all three relate to the same emotion. It is therefore not like Aristotle's pity or fear, a reaction or sequel to the experience. There is (for reasons that need not be gone into here) no tragedy in classical Sanskrit drama, but if it had accommodated tragedy, the tragic emotion would have been not pity for the sufferer in the play, but the suffering itself (*śoka*) developed into the *karuṇa rasa*.

When Sanskrit theory speaks of a single emotion dominating a dramatic or narrative poem, what is meant is obviously the emotion presented as resident in the central character, motivating the plot and informing the language and imagery of the poem. Eliot's analysis of the emotional motif of *Hamlet*, like his definition of the objective correlative, is entirely consonant with the *Rasa-dhvani* theory. The essential emotion of the play, as he sees it, is the emotion that dominates the Prince. This emotion, *bībhatsa* (disgust), and not pity or fear, is the dominant emotion of the play. The basic tragic emotion, *karuṇa*, is also at work, but it is not the supreme principle of the play as it is of *King Lear*.

The emotional quality of a poem is often determined by the emotional composition of its hero. Achilles and Jimmy Porter are 'hot, impatient, revengeful, *impiger, iracundus, inexorabilis, acer,* etc.' (to quote Dryden's summing up of the hero of the *Iliad*), and we have Homer's epic and Osborne's play, disparate in all else but both ruled by *raudra* (anger). (In the *Iliad*, *raudra* is reinforced with *vīra*, the heroic.) Aeneas is (so is Yudhiṣṭhira) 'patient, considerate, careful of his people, and merciful to his enemies; ever submissive to the will of heaven, *quo fata trahunt, retrahuntque, sequamur*' (Dryden's summing up again), and we have the *Aeneid* and the *Mahābhārata*, obeying an undercurrent of *śānta* (serenity).

But is it always as simple as that? Cannot a poem be telling at times of an experience that is not strictly emotional or is a mixture of affective and cognitive elements or is so complex and individual that it cannot be classified at all? It is, of course, idle to pretend that every poem, every line of a poem, is touched with one or the other of the primary emotions. But the point surely is that a poem which does not want to disintegrate into several poems or a play which does not want to ignore the fact of a theatre audience has to orient itself firmly to a final cumulative emotional impression. This may or may not be one of the traditional formulations but must essentially be felt as a distinct and integral experience. Sanskrit theory does not agree that the suggested meaning (whether it be emotion or any other form) can be obscure or indeterminate (*anirdeśya*).

One of the chief concerns of the *Rasa-dhvani* theory has been the study of how the other *rasa*s in a poem are organized round its dominant *rasa*. Some of the richest effects in poetry are wrought from the juxtaposition or alternation, the opposition or union, of different *rasa*s. The meaning of *Samson Agonistes*, for instance, lies less in theology or autobiography than in the contrapuntal employment of *vīra* (the heroic) and *karuṇa* (the pathetic). The *raison d'être* of the plot is to conduct Samson from sorrow (*śoka*, the base of *karuṇa*) to a reborn elation and ardour (*utsāha*, the base of *vīra*). From the plane of retrospective contemplation where it dwells in the poem, for it is alien to the realities of Samson's present, *vīra* acts upon the poem's chief emotion, *karuṇa* (the quality of the present), penetrating and assimilating it—though the mood at the actual close of the poem is *śānta* (calm). To describe the poem in these terms is not to dehumanize it but to unfold the design beneath the play of personalities and events. The point, similarly, of St Peter's speech in *Lycidas* is not that it is the customary dose of satire in a pastoral elegy nor that it is really Milton denouncing the contemporary clergy. It is undoubtedly both these, but its meaning, just where it is placed, lies in its note of *raudra* (indignation)—or is it *bībhatsa* (repugnance)?—which, by tension, reinforces the elegiac emotion (*karuṇa*) to whose tokens of graceful memorial tenderness we revert when the dread voice is past.

It seems presumptuous to take the floor in the Satan debate and then only to suggest that it need perhaps never have been started. Given that emotion supplies the conscious or unconscious design of poetry and that a whole poem is governed by a single emotion and different parts by different emotions, 'Satan, hero or fool?' is perhaps too simple a form in which to propound the question. The ruling emotion of a poem which tells how disobedience brought death into the world and all our woe is, of course, *karuṇa*. But the opening portions of the poem present a different woe—the Apostate Angel's deep despair—from which soon enough comes the blaze of high defiance. The dominant emotion of the first two books is the heroic (*vīra*), and Satan is, while it lasts, its chief objective equivalent. When Milton passes on to a different emotional key, Satan's heroic proportions inevitably shrink. Since consistency is to be defined not as continuing sameness in the character but as accord of character with emotion, the Archfiend 'rotting away' is a process of no interest to the *sahṛdaya*, the reader who seeks to be *en rapport* with the emotion.

A major problem of contemporary poetry and poetics is that of how a long poem in the strict Symbolist manner, composed exclusively of non-propositional imagery, can exist as a whole poem and not as a mere string of symbols. But the solution was presented when the problem itself was first presented in *The Waste Land*. *The Waste Land* is a disposition of symbols. It is also a long poem with as much unity as Aristotle or Ānandavardhana could have wished. Its inconsequential centrifugal images are held together by an underlying emotional unity—a single dominant *rasa* working as an undercurrent. It is impossible to identify the specific *rasa* of *The Waste Land* as one of the 'permanent emotions'. It is in fact impossible to find a name for it—Eliot's readers called it disillusionment, and Eliot thought it could be their own 'illusion of being disillusioned'. It is all the same a real enough emotion and constitutes the total meaning of the heterogeneous images that make up the poem. In the introduction to St John Perse's *Anabase*, Eliot himself confirms that 'the reader has to allow the images to fall into his memory successively without questioning the reasonableness of each at the moment, so that at the end, a total effect is produced'. The total effect is an emotional effect; as Richards says, speaking of some of Eliot's poems, ' . . . the items are united by the accord, contrast, and interaction of their emotional effects, not by an intellectual scheme that analysis must work out. The value lies in the unified response which this interaction creates in the right reader.'[16] In other words, emotion is structure.

4

The Lamp and the Jar: Stated and Suggested Meaning

One of I. A. Richards's more significant latter-day insights
—or recantations?—is the notion that prose (scientific
language, that is) is a questionable means of studying and
describing the not-prose and that metaphor can be seriously
used 'not as a literary grace, but as a technique of reflection and an operation of research'.[1] Curiously enough, the
thinking and talking about poetry that went on in Sanskrit
criticism did in fact turn upon crucial metaphors. The
Anvitābhidhāna theory of meaning used the metaphor of the
arrow; the theory of *Rasa* used, among other things, the
concoction of pepper, candy and camphor as a tool metaphor. But the 'founding metaphor',[2] to apply Richards's
phrase, of the central poetic in Sanskrit—the *Dhvani* Poetic
—is the lamp and the jar. The metaphor identifies the two
factors of suggestion as the suggestor and the suggested. On
the one hand, there is stated meaning, which is the suggestor;
and on the other, there is suggested meaning. The lamp is
stated meaning (*vācyārtha*); the jar is suggested meaning
(*vyangyārtha*) which it illuminates and reveals. The metaphor
was used by Sanskrit critics, although probably not quite
in the manner Richards has in mind, as an instrument for
analysing and describing the relationship and comparative
status of stated and suggested meaning. This, I think, is a

unique enquiry; a full-length study of poetic meaning as dual and hierarchical has not been, as far as I know, undertaken elsewhere. The explanation for this is the reign of certain other metaphors! ' . . . A Swedish drill, in which nothing is being lifted, transported, or set down, though the muscles tense, knot, and relax as if it were' (Donald Davie, explaining Susanne Langer's theory);[3] the 'bit of nice meat for the house-dog' that 'the imaginary burglar is always provided with' (T. S. Eliot)[4]—stated meaning, as these metaphors used for describing it show, is often looked upon as an illusion or as a diversion, and the attitude has inhibited any serious study of the stated and the suggested as the two dimensions of meaning. Another obstacle has been terminology. The word 'meaning' is sometimes used to denote what is stated—as in F. W. Bateson's summing up of the Suggestion Theory: ' . . . poetry is not concerned with what words mean but with what they suggest. A good poem apparently should mean very little while suggesting a great deal.'[5] 'Meaning' at other times is made to denote what is suggested, as when John Bayley speaks of searching for Dylan Thomas's meaning and equates it with 'a concealed significance'.[6] Worst of all, 'meaning' can be used to denote stated meaning one moment and suggested meaning the next, as when T. S. Eliot, within the space of 28 lines, first speaks of meaning as explicit prose discourse and then refers to 'a meaning which reveals itself gradually' in Shakespeare's plays.[7]

Such inadequacy of terminology can frustrate any comparative study of stated and suggested meaning. But a more serious obstacle is the view that the dichotomy is unreal and that meaning is one and indivisible. To return to John Bayley on Dylan Thomas, he deprecates conscious ex-

ploration of suggested meaning and says: 'There is no gap—
no intellectually sensible gap that is—between our grasping of
the words and our deduction of what they are supposed to
stand for.'[8] To be sure, according to Sanskrit theory, there
is *in practice* no gap between the grasping of the statement
and the grasping of the emotive meaning suggested; that is
to say, the mind leaps it so instantly that the gap is not
sensible (*asaṁlakṣya*) and the two meanings—the stated and
the suggested—are perceived almost simultaneously. Almost
but not quite—because essentially the apprehension of suggested meaning succeeds (however imperceptible the stages
of succession) the apprehension of stated meaning. In perception, the two meanings are almost one; in description,
however, they can very properly be treated as distinct
elements. We have after all (to use Pater's phrase) an
achieved distinction here, and there is nothing to be gained
by obliterating it. On the contrary, viewing statement and
suggestion as separate entities and analysing their mutual relation might help to light up much that is obscure and con-
fusing in the emergence of poetic meaning.

But we might be deepening the confusion instead if we
do not begin by defining the term 'statement'. 'Statement',
as used in this chapter, means literal or stated meaning
treated as one component of a *suggestive* poem, the other
component being suggested meaning. In a later chapter I
will be using 'statement' to mean whole poems (or portions
of them) that are *non-suggestive*. As an explanation, if not as
an excuse, for this verbal looseness, I can plead that 'statement', like 'meaning', is an instance of inadequacy of
critical terminology. I can also plead that I am not alone
here. Tillyard, for instance, in the very act of defining what
makes 'The Deserted Village' and 'The Echoing Green'

specimens of two opposed kinds of poetry describes 'The Deserted Village' as statement poetry and speaks of the statement in 'The Echoing Green'![9] Sanskrit has separate terms for the two uses of the word 'statement'. The first 'statement' (i.e. discursive poetry) is *citrakāvya*; the second (i.e. stated meaning) is *vācyārtha*. In this chapter I use the word in the latter sense—the sense which the lamp *vis-à-vis* the jar denotes.

The use of the lamp-jar metaphor as an instrument of reflection in ninth-century Sanskrit criticism yielded several insights into the behaviour of the stated and suggested components of meaning when the suggested component is emotion and the stated component is its objective correlatives. Into their behaviour, that is, as observed in contemporary or earlier Sanskrit poetry, so that it can't be claimed for these findings that they have universal applicability. But some of them might prove useful in re-examining, in present-day terms, the relationship of stated and suggested meaning; and in attempting this we will not be quite so much describing these findings as using them as points of departure for an independent study.

In the first place, *the jar was already there, the lamp only revealed it*. The lamp and the jar are a conventional formula in Indian philosophy for stating the theory of manifestation. Applied to poetry, the theory sees the process of suggestion as the revealing of what is already there rather than as the presenting of anything new. 'What is already there'—one is reminded of the remark in Empson's *Seven Types*: ' . . . Being an essentially suggestive act it (poetry) can only take effect if the impulses (and to some extent the experiences) are already there to be called forth; that the process of getting to understand a poet is precisely that of constructing

E

his poems in one's own mind.'[10] It is clear that Empson is thinking here of reader participation as a factor of suggestion, and this, of course, is a different thing from the ontological recognition (embodied in the lamp-jar formula) of the nature of suggestion as identical with the nature of manifestation. All the same, the principle of reader participation can be looked at in terms of the lamp and the jar—the stated meaning, when the reader makes contact with it, acts upon an existing capacity within him for response to symbolized emotion, and the suggested meaning is rendered manifest in his consciousness. Sanskrit theory, as we saw in the last chapter, assumes that when the sensuous correlates of the emotion activate one of the emotional sets latent in the reader, the supreme aesthetic response is evoked. It also assumes that only the reader whom nature or nurture has equipped with a special sensibility can respond in this way. As Lascelles Abercrombie says, ' . . . the author must rely on his readers' ability to respond to what his language can only suggest . . . It is the sense of language, proved by ability to respond to the suggestions of language, that makes the enjoyer of literary art.'[11] This type of reader goes to work actively on the poem—on this showing, being illuminated is not a passive rôle for the jar but an energetic act of response.

The second observed feature of the lamp-jar relationship is that *the lamp continues to shine even after the jar has been illuminated.* To class statement as stuff which gets used up in the generation of suggested meaning, as something that disappears from, or can be dismissed from, our thoughts when it has served its purpose is to misread the process of suggestion. Even when the suggested meaning has been apprehended, the stated meaning is intact and continues to be active. Sanskrit critics thus saw statement as non-expendable, except where metaphor is present and supersedes, as it must (according to them), the stated meaning. (We will return in the next chapter to the action of metaphor on statement.) Where the stated meaning consists in the objective correlatives of the emotion, these, far from being superseded, continue to exist—in fact, they suggest the emotion by themselves developing rapidly into it. The granite shore, the white sails and the cry of quail are not banished from our consciousness when the mood that *Ash Wednesday* evokes through them has been realized—they persist and are integral with the mood.

But the mood can fail to get realized if its correlatives are inadequately or ineptly presented. When T. S. Eliot speaks of lack of 'explicit reference of emotion to object',[12] or lack of 'adequacy of the external to the emotion',[13] he is in fact referring to inadequacy of statement; and when he calls *Hamlet* a failure, he means that it is a failure of statement. And this brings us to the third observation: *the lamp not only reveals the jar but reveals itself*. It could not establish the identity of the jar if in the very act of doing so it didn't establish its own, asserting its own solidity, presenting itself as a bright clear object. Eliot too—and here is a remarkable coincident insight—defines the relation between stated and suggested meaning in terms of a light: '. . . suggestiveness is the aura around a bright clear centre.'[14] In order to have the aura (the suggested meaning), you must have a bright clear centre (the stated meaning). In order to illuminate the jar the lamp must also illuminate itself.

Sanskrit theory makes the point that, strictly speaking, the suggested meaning is apprehended, despite the apparent simultaneity, *after* the stated meaning and indeed through it and is governed by it. Language, we may add, cannot suggest unless it has first stated, and then what it stated is the base which supports what it suggests. Sanskrit criticism calls this *vācyārthāpekṣā* (dependence on stated meaning). As F. W. Bateson points out, if you don't know where Troy is and what happened there, you can't respond to the suggested meaning in Yeats's line, 'Troy passed away in one high funeral gleam'.[15] This, of course, is but common sense—the least we owe the poet is to begin by reading what he wrote and understanding his plain meaning. If we neglect to do this, we are in danger of erring as egregiously as Edith Sitwell did when Dylan Thomas's 'Atlas-eater with a jaw for news', who 'bit out the mandrake with tomorrow's scream' from the gentleman's fork, was taken by her as referring to the modern craze for speed, horror and sensation. As John Bayley explains, she ignored the verb 'bit out'; no wonder Thomas complained, 'She doesn't take the literal meaning'.[16] When statement is read perfunctorily (as in this case) or is tenuous and inchoate (as in some Romantic poetry) or tortured and unintelligible (as in some Symbolist and Post-Symbolist poetry), suggestion is aborted.

It is, of course, true that if inadequacy of statement can abort suggestion, so can perfect adequacy of statement—in a different way. This is a very necessary qualification to attach to the *vācyārthāpekṣā* concept. Where the stated meaning is self-contained and sufficient, it doesn't compel reference to anything beyond itself so that any further meaning found is more a bonus added than a need met. To return to F. W. Bateson, he finds in Herrick's 'A Sweet Disorder in the Dress' a covert plea for pagan morals and manners. He arrives at this interpretation by taking the human adjectives applied by the poet to features of dress and referring them back to the wearer.[17] It is an attractive interpretation, and if its authority seems to be less than adequate, it is because the poem can be read quite satisfyingly as no more than an elegant compliment to a girl's charm which only gains by any carelessness in dress; there is nothing in the poem to oblige us to get beyond this meaning which is by itself sufficient and entire. Compare Herrick's poem with Roethke's 'I Knew a Woman':

> Love likes a gander, and adores a goose:
> Her full lips pursed, the errant note to seize;
> She played it quick, she played it light and loose;
> My eyes, they dazzled at her flowing knees;
> Her several parts could keep a pure repose,
> Or one hip quiver with a mobile nose
> (She moved in circles, and those circles moved).

Unlike so much poetry that uses deformation of syntax as an instrument of suggestion, these lines are syntactically regular, but all their other features—the logical discontinuity, the discrete images, the incongruity of certain collocations—serve to make the statement incapable of standing on its own legs; the suggested meaning thus becomes an imperative need. Where, on the contrary, the statement is independent and self-supporting, it always usurps the dominant rôle, and we have (for a different reason from what Sanskrit theory had in view when it coined the phrase) 'the poetry of subordinate suggestion'.

Whether the deriving of suggested meaning from the stated is not after all a form of logical inference was the subject of a lengthy debate which the *Dhvani* theorists had to fight and win before suggestion was accepted as a substantive mode. And it isn't as though these schoolmen went

on sharpening their teeth on each other over an exquisitely
bookish point. The distinction between deduction and suggestion is not always as obvious as one would think. We
are all close readers today and tend to be cerebral, so that in
expounding the unstated meaning of a poem we are not
above cheating—we can, that is to say, catch ourselves
offering a deduction wrapped and labelled as a suggestion.
Or we can find ourselves syllogizing unabashedly, as Pound
did, commenting on a Li Po piece translated by himself:

N.B.

> The jewelled steps are already quite white with dew,
>   It is so late that the dew soaks my gauze stockings . . .

Pound's gloss is: 'Jewel stairs, therefore a palace . . . Gauze
stockings, therefore a court lady . . .'[18] But no cast-iron
'because—therefore' can make us move inexorably from
'jewelled steps' to 'a palace'—jewelled steps could equally
legitimately suggest street lights on a steep rise, a starry sky
or a bedecked bosom. This brings us to the fourth finding:
the lamp and the jar are not necessarily found together. Inference
is based on the invariable concomitance of the middle term
and the major term; stated and suggested meaning have no
such relationship. Yet another statement possible about the
lamp and the jar is that although the jar gets lighted up after
the lamp has started giving off light, the interval is too
minute to be noticeable. A conclusion follows a premise by
perceptible succession marked by mediacy; on the other
hand, the illuminator-illuminable relation which governs
stated and suggested meaning is based on immediate and
imperceptible succession. The work of our best close readers
shows that they arrive at the further meaning by association
and not by inference. From Nash's line 'Brightness falls
from the air', Empson derives the meaning that the earth is

brighter than the sky when the clouds are dark and there is a threat of thunder.[19] This, although ingenious, is not a logical conclusion, for Empson derives several other possible meanings from the same line. From the words 'cannot scare' in Frost's line, 'They cannot scare me with their empty spaces', Cleanth Brooks and R. P. Warren obtain the meaning that the speaker is a mature man.[20] This is not inferring the state of being a child from the state of being scared; it is just selecting one of the connotational meanings of 'scared'.

Ninth-to-eleventh-century Sanskrit criticism produced a considerable body of theory not only about the relation of stated to suggested meaning but also about their comparative status. Its main assumption, reduced to very simple terms, is that stated meaning should be subordinate and suggested meaning supreme: supreme by virtue of its aesthetic worth and also by virtue of its exclusive importance (which implies, I suppose, that stated meaning should have no importance whatever except as suggestor). Suggestive poetry strictly so called is where the suggested meaning is paramount; where it is not paramount, we have merely guṇībhūtavyaṅgya, 'the poetry of subordinate suggestion'. The principle, stated in such general terms, seems unexceptionable, but when its exponents proceed to apply it to a given passage, one finds that the grounds on which they determine the status of the suggested meaning with reference to its beauty and importance tend to be arbitrary, or at any rate unclear. Nevertheless it might be useful, quite independently of Sanskrit criticism (although we will probably find ourselves returning to it often), to try to devise guide lines for determining the status of suggested in relation to stated meaning.

Suggested meaning reigns assuredly supreme when it consists in an emotion or mood as distinct from an idea.

Now this is, I am afraid, a coarse distinction worthy of the young Yeats who spoke of symbols that 'evoke emotion alone' and intellectual ones that 'evoke ideas alone'.[21] As Cleanth Brooks and R. P. Warren point out, ' . . . a mood implies an idea, as an idea implies a mood'.[22] Yet it is perhaps a distinction that embodies a real enough difference. The point is that in a poem the mood created has necessarily more authority than the sensuous details through which it is created. The emotion-meaning suggested is essentially the dominant principle in relation to the stated meaning, because the objects presented descriptively are the correlates of the emotion and cannot possibly outshine it without repudiating their own nature. But when it is an idea, and not an emotion, that is being evoked, the statement, I think, can acquire an autonomous interest and dwarf what is suggested. This can easily happen when an image develops so much intensity and vigour that the idea of which it is the concretion is quite overshadowed. This is the price Auden is sometimes found paying for the nightmarish brightness, the cinemato-graphic vividness, of his images:

> For the wicked card is dealt, and
> The sinister tall-hatted botanist stoops at the spring
> With his insignificant phial and looses
> The plague on the ignorant town.
>
> ('Epilogue' in *Look, Stranger*)

Sanskrit critics would call this 'the poetry of subordinate suggestion'. Poe would have called it 'the poetry of the fancy', adding: 'Here the upper current is often exceedingly brilliant and beautiful; but then men *feel* that this upper current is *all*.' If what Auden suggests in these lines is the rôle of science as destroyer of civilization, the Hitchcockian effect succeeds only in focussing attention on itself and the idea suggested is cast into the shade. In *New Year Letter*, Auden arrives at the idea that there is a fearful price to be paid if we try to prolong the momentary mystic release from Becoming into Being:

> He hears behind his back the wicket
> Padlock itself, from the dark thicket
> The chuckle with no healthy cause,
> And helpless, sees the crooked claws
> Emerging into view and groping
> For handholds on the low round coping,
> As Horror clambers from the well.

The picture is, at a lowbrow level if you like, so arresting that what is suggested can't hope to compete with what is said. Earlier in the same poem, Auden offers a sort of microfilm projecting the universal spiritual guilt of our time:

> There lies the body half-undressed,
> We all had reason to detest,
> And all are suspects and involved
> Until the mystery is solved
> And under lock and key the cause
> That makes a nonsense of our laws.
> O Who is trying to shield Whom?
> Who left a hairpin in the room?
> Who was the distant figure seen
> Behaving oddly on the green?
> Why did the watchdog never bark?
> Why did the footsteps leave no mark?
> Where were the servants at that hour?
> How did a snake get in the tower?

The situation, wrapped in evil and enigma, is elaborated with some gusto; the features, which have no individual allegorical reference, add up to a total effect which, although merely Agatha-Christian, is of such compelling vividness that the concept suggested is quite eclipsed.

Like Auden's glowing images, some of Ted Hughes's fauna—the tom cat, the too dead pig, the too slow bull—are unforgettable studies that we start caring for for their own sake, and they seem to be more important than any human implication that can be assigned to them. Yeats's haunting image of the rough beast slouching in the sand amid the desert birds clearly matters more to us than anything it could be suggesting, and so does Shelley's Magus Zoroaster who 'met his own image walking in the garden'. Eliot's

> another one walking beside you
> Gliding wrapped in a brown mantle, hooded
> I do not know whether a man or a woman...
>
> (*The Waste Land*)

is yet another image that states too vividly. I am not sure this is always to be treated as a flaw. 'The symbol,' says Tindall, 'is more important than what it suggests...'[23] The self-validating symbol risen from the unconscious was alien to the daylight beauty and order of classical Sanskrit poetry on which the ninth-century theory of poetry was reared; the presentation of identifiable emotion through its traditionally associated objects was more in its line, and it naturally saw as poetically vital not the symbol that tries to present an experience, or maybe outshines it in so trying, but the emotion that is evoked by its object.

Apart from the dazzling statement that steals the show, there is another condition that can lower the status of suggested meaning. This is a condition frequently encountered in poetry given to explicitness: what has been suggested is also stated, and inevitably the spelling out reduces the potency of the utterance. Take the following lines from Gascoyne's 'A Wartime Dawn':

> Draw now with prickling hand the curtains back;
> Unpin the blackout-cloth; let in
> Grim crack-of-dawn's first glimmer through the glass.
> All's yet half-sunk in Yesterday's stale death,
> Obscurely still beneath a moist-tinged blank
> Sky like the inside of a deaf mute's mouth . . .
> Nearest within the window's sight, ash-pale
> Against a cinder-coloured wall, the white
> Pearblossom hovers like a stare; rain-wet
> The further housetops weakly shine; and there,
> Beyond, hangs flaccidly a lone barrage-balloon.
>
> An incommunicable desolation weighs
> Like depths of stagnant water on this break of day . . .

The passage first calls up a mood through evocative land-scape, but the last two lines, which are a statement of the mood, succeed in depressing the status of the suggested meaning. To realize how disastrously they succeed, one has only to compare Gascoyne's description with Eliot's pre-sentation of the same hour in 'Preludes' where a like mood of desolation is evoked through descriptive detail but left unnamed.

By calling the last two lines from Gascoyne a statement, I am afraid I have committed the same offence that I charged Dr Tillyard with at the beginning of this chapter—that of simultaneously using the term 'statement' in its two different senses. In this chapter we have been examining suggested meaning in relation to statement-as-suggestor (which is what the first eleven lines from Gascoyne are) and not in relation to explicit statement (which is what the last two lines are). Yet we can't help concerning ourselves with the latter—because the point made here is that when a poem has presented a mood by suggestion, explication deprives the suggested meaning of its dominant rôle in relation to the stated meaning. That a symbol suggests what by its nature can never be stated is a familiar law of modern Western aesthetics; ninth-century Sanskrit critics were able to anticipate it. That they could do so without having known the principle of symbol is, I think, a remarkable achievement of insight.

5

Suggestion through Metaphor

An interesting finding of the imagery studies of recent years is the distinction between the image which makes a point, directs your attention to the specific relation between the two terms of the metaphor, and the image which works by suggestion, by the radiation of a quantity of multiple imprecise meaning—between the stiff twin compasses and the sick rose. The two are treated as mutually exclusive kinds, labelled, and even identified with periods. ' . . . The metaphysicals and the modernists stand opposed to the neoclassic and Romantic poets on the issue of metaphor,' says Cleanth Brooks.[1] 'The making of a point, the outlining of a picture, as opposed to that suggestiveness of image which is the aim of the contemporary poet, as it was of the Romantics and often of the Elizabethan dramatists, is the keynote of Augustan imagery,' says Cecil Day Lewis.[2] So where are we? Is Augustan imagery (which 'makes a point', according to Day Lewis) akin to Metaphysical imagery (which also does, according to Rosemond Tuve) or to Romantic imagery (which, along with Augustan, eschews the play of the intellect, according to Cleanth Brooks)? Is the modernist image sprung from the Romantic image (as Read and Kermode show) or from the Metaphysical image (as several others show)? And do Elizabethan metaphors suggest, or do they make a point?

Obviously, dividing imagery into two kinds and linking them with periods scarcely helps. The value of Allen Tate's theory of 'tension' lies in its demonstration of the truth that it is only in bad poetry that imagery is exclusively 'extensive' (denotative) or exclusively 'intensive' (connotative or suggestive).[3] Specificity either of statement or of metaphor, on the one hand, and richness of suggestion, on the other, are the two poles in all poetry, and every poet starts at either end and works towards the other, and if he pushes far enough but not too far, achieves 'tension'. The only difference between the Metaphysical and the Romantic is that they start at different ends of the scale, the extensive and the intensive—but their goal is the same: the point of tension. Metaphor and suggestion thus, far from being two categories of imagery, are two co-present functions at work within an image.

Co-present, but always distinct. The operation of metaphor proper—consisting ostensibly in the establishment of the logical relationship of the primary and secondary referents and in the vehicle's illumination of the tenor—is distinct from the accompanying emergence of imprecise expansible meaning. Indeed the latter can often be independent of the metaphor and vastly more important. 'More usually,' says I. A. Richards, 'the elucidation is a mere pretence . . . There are few metaphors whose effect, if carefully examined, can be traced to the logical relations involved. Metaphor is a semi-surreptitious method by which a greater variety of elements can be wrought into the fabric of the experience.'[4] Others too have noticed the same curious phenomenon. 'In understanding imaginative metaphor we are required to consider not how B (vehicle) explains A (tenor), but what meanings are generated when A and B are confronted or seen each in the light of the other . . . ', says Wimsatt, explaining Martin Foss's theory of metaphor; and he quotes Foss as saying about the proverb 'Among blind men the one-eyed is king': 'The true significance of the proverb goes far beyond the blind, the one-eyed, and the king: it points to a wisdom in regard to which the terms of comparison are only unimportant cases of reference.'[5] (An interesting parallel case of suggested meaning being independent of the image is Archibald MacLeish's 'coupled images'. When two unrelated images (such as a bracelet of bright hair and a bone) are juxtaposed, ' . . . a meaning appears which is neither the meaning of one image nor the meaning of the other nor even the sum of both but a *consequence* of both—a consequence of both in their conjunction, in their relation to each other.'[6] This, of course, is different from what happens in a metaphor. In a metaphor the two terms are linked.) To return to Richards, explaining his notion that 'metaphor supplies an excuse by which what is needed may be smuggled in'—an application to metaphor of his theory that in poetry referential elements are only a means to the evocation of attitudes and are in themselves relatively unimportant—Richards speaks of a mysterious effect in art: an essential or important thing is said best if it is said not overtly and evidently but apparently inadvertently, as a by-product or an accidental concomitant.[7] This is an important principle behind suggestion, but it throws no light on why metaphor often accompanies or precedes suggestion and whether and how metaphor serves suggestion. How is it that the complex meanings which surface around or in the wake of the metaphor are more important than the metaphor and apparently independent of it and indeed turn out to be the poet's real concern?

Part of the answer seems available in Sanskrit poetics, which distinguishes three chief meaning-functions of language—statement (*abhidhā*), metaphor (*lakṣaṇā*), and suggestion (*vyañjanā*). Metaphor, according to Sanskrit poetics and philosophy, occurs when the primary referent of the word is found incompatible with the intended sense in the context, and to remove the incongruity (*mukhyārthabādha*), meaning is transferred to a secondary referent connected with the primary one by similarity or some other relationship. The primary referent must be found incompatible with the context; the secondary referent must be related to the primary one; the transfer of meaning must have the sanction either of usage (*rūḍhi*) or of the specific purpose or use (*prayojana*) of the metaphor—these are the three basic conditions of metaphor. In Donne's line from 'The Autumnal'

I shall ebb out with them, who home-ward go

the primary referent of 'ebb' is (for the tide) 'to flow back' and is inapplicable to a human being; so a secondary referent (let us say 'ageing'—when it is poetry you are dealing with, secondary referents are at best clumsy substitutes) has to be found. This transfer of meaning is 'sanctioned' or motivated by the poet's intention to suggest the serenity of love in late life.* On the other hand, the historian's cliché in 'The fortunes of the Eighth Army ebbed rapidly' is sanctioned by usage. Naturally, the incompatibility (*anupapatti*) of the primary reference is more pronounced in an intentional or created metaphor (*prayojanavatī-lakṣaṇā*)—created, as mostly happens, by a poet—than in a conventional metaphor em-

---

*Wellek and Warren in their *Theory of Literature* (p. 196) refer to Wilhelm Wundt's notion that 'the calculated, willed intention of its user to create an emotive effect' is the criterion of true or poetic metaphor.

bedded in usage (*nirūḍha-lakṣaṇā*) where the primary reference is faded. Why does a poet create a metaphor? The
raison d'être or purpose or use of the metaphor—that is to
say, what caused it at the poet's end; what results from it, at
the reader's—is revealed or apprehended by the process of
suggestion. Thus Donne's metaphor, having established the
relation between ebbing and ageing, goes on to suggest the
unstrenuous serenity of love in late life, almost indistinguish-
able from easy dissolution; and working associatively it links
itself with the earlier metaphor:

> may still
> My love descend and journey down the hill.

Of the meaning of a passage containing a metaphor, just as
much as is needed for removing the incompatibility of the
primary reference is the metaphorical or secondary meaning
—the rest is suggested meaning.

> Let me pour forth
> My tears before thy face, whil'st I stay here,
> For thy face coins them, and thy stamp they bear,
> And by this Mintage they are something worth ...
> ('A Valediction: Of Mourning')

In the last two lines as they stand, the numismatic terms, on
the one hand, and the lover's tears and the mistress's face,
on the other, are in conflict with each other. When we
render the meaning of the lines as 'Because my tears will
reflect your face and thus acquire value', we are offering the
metaphorical meaning which resolves the disharmony. But
Donne's lines have a large residue of suggested meaning—
in beauty and worth and in her power over him, the mistress
is as a queen; there is also the tragic paradox of the currency
(what can be more permanent than something stamped on

F

metal?) lasting only while she is physically before him. There are, similarly, the legal metaphors in Shakespeare's lines:

> The Charter of thy worth gives thee releasing;
> My bonds in thee are all determinate.
>
> (Sonnet 87)

When the primary references of the legal terms are superseded and the secondary or metaphorical meaning of the lines given, their meaning is far from exhausted. There is an envelope of suggested meaning left: the irony of running an intimate emotion into absolute impersonal moulds; the seal of heart-breaking irrevocability which the definitive language of law sets on the parting; and maybe much else. This, rather than the metaphoric point, must be what made Shakespeare employ legal imagery here. And here, as in Donne's lines, the suggested meaning is more or less independent of the metaphoric point.

The nuances and insights of this relatively unspecific suggested meaning are beyond the language of metaphor. Poetic metaphor thus leads to and fulfils itself in suggestion, but the two are distinct functions. When the apparent incompatibility of the vehicle with the context is corrected by linking it to the tenor, the function of metaphor has exhausted itself. The comparatively imprecise and fluid meaning through which the purpose or use of the metaphor manifests itself is extraneous to metaphor. There are many more reasons why suggestion cannot be treated as part of metaphor. Metaphor is based on the primary meaning, it is the primary meaning transferred, extended; suggestion, as in music, can occur in the absence of the primary meaning. Metaphor supersedes the primary meaning; suggestion exists alongside of it. Metaphor succeeds the primary meaning; the primary meaning and the suggested meaning arise almost (almost, though not quite, as we saw in the last chapter) simultaneously, as when a poem suggests an emotion by stating its objective correlatives. Metaphor specifies an idea, a logical relation; suggestion is imprecise, indeterminate, accessible through interpretation, and dependent on such variables as the writer, the reader, the context . . . These four or five sentences read rather like an undergraduate's notes and make the whole thing look too easy, but no summary can do justice to the formidable body of theory thrown up by that long shrill debate in Sanskrit poetics: Is suggestion distinct from metaphor?

The notion of 'Semantic Synthesis' propounded by F. W. Bateson is an attempt (analogous to Mukulabhaṭṭa's in Sanskrit which did not find acceptance) to subsume suggestion under metaphor.[8] 'Incantation' or 'verbal magic' is to Bateson the collocation and reconciliation of apparently unconnected, even contrasted or conflicting, units of meaning. Chaucer's line

> Ne how the ground agast was of the light
> > (*The Knight's Tale*)

was to Lascelles Abercrombie a triumph of suggestion—the 'release, even from common words, of uncommon energy of meaning'. Bateson finds that the effect is simply that of a metaphor yoking fear and the insentient forest ground. The so-called suggested sense, as he sees it, is no mysterious exhalation that has a life of its own independent of the metaphor, but a clear cognizable meaning produced by the bridging of the 'semantic gap' between the two disparates brought together in the metaphor. This is a corollary of

Bateson's view that suggestion, understood as the opposite of finite precise meaning, is a principle that has little relevance outside Romantic poetry. Sanskrit poetics, on the other hand, holds that suggestion is the highest mode of utterance in any kind of poetry whatever and also, as we saw, that suggestion is distinct from metaphor. It in fact recognizes a form of suggestion that is based on metaphor (*lakṣaṇāmūladhvani*) (which is what we have been examining) and a form that is based not on metaphoric but on primary meaning (*abhidhāmūladhvani*). The former is also termed *avivakṣitavācya* ('where the stated meaning is not meant'), for metaphor operates by replacing the primary with a secondary meaning. The latter form of suggestion, which we dealt with in the last two chapters, is called *vivakṣitānyaparavācya* ('where the stated meaning is meant and resolves itself into another—the suggested—meaning'). This form consists largely, if not entirely, in the suggestion of emotion, the stated meaning being made up of the objective correlatives and the suggested meaning being the emotion itself.

An altogether remarkable parallel insight makes Sir Herbert Read formulate the very same distinction—between metaphoric suggestion and suggestion of emotion.[9] An example he gives of the former is Tennyson's line,

> Now lies the Earth all Danaë to the stars.
> (*The Princess*)

For the other kind of suggestion—'simple statements devoid of metaphor' offering visual details which 'have the power of evoking the full reality in all its emotional significance'— Read gives as an example Shelley's lyric, 'A widow bird sate mourning for her love', which presents grief (*śoka*) suggestively through its objective correlatives.

The Sanskrit theory of poetic metaphor, as we have seen, sets it in a three-tier meaning structure:

Vācyārtha. The literal meaning, thwarted by the incongruity between the word's primary referent and the context. This is what happens in Hart Crane's lines

> The dice of drowned men's bones he saw bequeath
> An embassy.

>   ('At Melville's Tomb')

The incongruity stung Harriet Monroe into writing and asking Hart Crane how dice could bequeath an embassy.[10]

Lakṣyārtha. The metaphorical or secondary meaning, obtained by substituting for the primary referent a secondary referent related to it. We thus effect transfer of meaning, relate the vehicle to the tenor and paraphrase the poetic metaphor—fatally. Hart Crane did this to his own metaphors when he cleared Harriet Monroe's puzzlement. 'The dice of drowned men's bones' became 'drowned men's bones ground into little cubes by the action of the sea'; 'bequeath an embassy' became 'washed ashore and offering evidence of messages about their experiences that the mariners might have had to deliver if they had survived'.

Vyaṅgyārtha. Alongside of these two levels of meaning is a third—suggested meaning—through which the purpose or use of the metaphor becomes manifest. Hart Crane explained that he had employed the metaphor of dice as it was 'a symbol of chance and circumstance'. This raises—or widens—the significance of the metaphor from the mere shape of the eroded bones to the whole ethos of Moby Dick's world.

The Sanskrit account of metaphor is of twofold interest. First, it treats metaphor and suggestion not as the principles of two types of image but as functions active in the same image. Secondly, it answers partly the question we started with: Why does metaphor seem to have more to it than the transfer and why is it found offering a bonus of meaning which turns out to be the poet's principal concern?

But the question is answered only partly. The Sanskrit version of the metaphor phenomenon, by assuming a neat removal of the literal meaning, has missed the fact that the metaphor draws its sustenance from the obstinate vitality, the unassimilable integrity, of the vehicle. In fact, suggested meaning, which is very important to metaphor as seen by Sanskrit analysts, most often springs from the incongruous literal meaning. W. B. Stanford, who has offered, I think, the best modern definition of metaphor, emphasizes the fact that A and B (what we have been calling the primary and secondary referents), though synthesized, 'retain their conceptual independence'.[11] A is not superseded; the incongruity is not fully removed. Indeed if it were removed, if the two terms of the metaphor existed in a state of fusion either because the analogy was perfect or because (as in a dead metaphor) A had been nicely absorbed into B, the metaphor would suffer inanition. The vigour of the metaphor lies in the very inadequacy of the similarity, in the unresolved or partially resolved tension of disparates. 'Some similarity', says I. A. Richards, 'will commonly be the ostensive ground of the shift, but the peculiar modification of the tenor which the vehicle brings about is even more the work of their unlikenesses than of their likenesses.'[12] Whether it is Aristotle's 'intuitive perception of the similarity in dissimilars', or Coleridge's 'balance or reconcilement of opposite or discordant qualities', or Eliot's 'amalgamating disparate experience', the important factor is not the drawing together of the two, but the continuing otherness of each. The vehicle and the tenor are brought close enough to each other to effect their mutual confrontation—and no closer. The vehicle not only maintains its distinctness and distance from, or even opposition to, the tenor but often becomes the more important—or even the only important—component of the metaphor. The vehicle is the creative part that the metaphor owes to what Freud called 'the never failing source of all art'—the unconscious. It is the vehicle that links itself with other vehicles in the poem to form themes and patterns and to give the poem its coherence and depth. The vehicle, its original reference intact, its identity inviolate, reigns supreme within the metaphor—and its relation to the tenor and its congruity with the context are ever imperfect. The vehicle disrupts the statement and arrests attention. 'To shock the audience by the violence and inadequacy of the analogy' (as Martin Foss says, speaking of the 'sick simile')[13] is the true function of metaphor. Its premises being what they are, the Sanskrit theory of metaphor, while admitting the fact of this shock, refrains from assigning any function to it and in fact provides for its quick resolution. Sanskrit poetics, like the classical poetry and the court drama from which it is evolved, is firmly committed to coherence and intelligibility. To us, however, the finding of a secondary meaning to remove the incongruity is but the establishing of rational meaning. The first tier (the disrupted statement) is the poem; the second (the meaning as it stands when the mess is cleared) is the paraphrase. Most of us would regard the latter as unimportant if not illegitimate. The shock is the thing.

The incongruity in what is being said pricks us into an awareness that more is meant than is being said, and we are laid open to the richer intimations that follow. The clash of vehicle and context has the effect of damaging the walls enclosing the meaning and it soon forces its way out, creating conditions of flux and diffusion in which its less precise and rigid elements, comprehensively called 'suggestion', can operate freely. This, I think, is how the shock works—it breaks the spell of logical discourse and renders the reader's mind receptive to the circumambient suggestion.

Distinguishing between metaphor and transfer and linking metaphor with equation and pregnancy, Empson in *The Structure of Complex Words*[14] refers to Gustav Stern's ideas:

Stern in *Meaning and Change of Meaning* distinguishes true metaphor as intentional, emotive, dependent on context, and accompanied by 'psychic resistance' ... it seems to me that his 'intentional, emotive, and dependent on context', so far as they are justified, all follow from his 'psychic resistance'. The thing is felt as a sort of break in the flow, requiring interpretation, exciting attention and perhaps other feelings.

Empson proceeds to redefine psychic resistance as resistance not to a remote analogy but to a false identity. The fact that by accepting the false identity you may 'fall into nonsense' stimulates you into interpreting it, into 'typifying' the vehicle (that is to say, concentrating on such characteristics of it as are typical and essential for the case in hand) so that 'pregnancy' results. A transfer offers no such difficulty and imposes no need for typifying. 'The rose of metaphor is an ideal rose, which involves a variety of vague suggestions and probably does not involve thorns, but the leaf of transfer is merely leafish.' Empson sums up the whole process thus:

It seems to me that what we start from, in a metaphor as distinct from a transfer, is a recognition that 'false identity' is being used, a feeling of 'resistance' to it, rather like going into higher gear, because the machinery of interpretation must be brought into play, and then a feeling of richness about the possible interpretations of the word . . .

This version—that the resistance to the incongruity or the danger of nonsense stimulates the reader to attend to the richer interpretable meaning—corroborates our assumption that the shock and the suggested meaning are related.[15]

Unless we keep the literal from the metaphorical meaning and watch the disruptive action of metaphor on statement (which is what yields the shock), we will not be able to account for the emergence of the 'intensive' meaning. Allen Tate's essay on 'Tension in Poetry' ends with an interpretation of the 'intensive' meaning of Francesca's words to Dante who finds her and Paolo whirling in the winds of lust:[16]

> Siede la terra dove nata fui
>> Sulla marina dove il Po discende
> Per aver pace co' seguaci sui.

(The town where I was born sits on the shore where the Po descends to be at peace with his pursuers.)

The Po, says Allen Tate, is Francesca herself; the tributaries are the winds of lust which while pursuing her merge in her, the sins merging in the sinner, even as the tributaries merge in the river; the sibilants in the last line where the tributaries are referred to complete the identification of tributaries and hissing winds. This is brilliantly perceptive, but by what process did all this meaning arise? 'For although Francesca has told Dante where she lives, in the most directly descriptive language possible, she has told him more than that,' says Allen Tate, stopping short of the explanation by millimetres. What has awakened us to the 'more than that' is the disruption of the 'directly descriptive language' by the metaphor for tributaries: *seguaci*. *Seguaci* is 'pursuers', and Tate condemns Courtney Landon's translation of the word as 'the streams that follow him'. This is paraphrasing, not translating—Landon offers the secondary meaning, having clipped off the incongruity of the metaphor-word ('pursuers') before the English reader can see it and be shocked. It is only when Tate has restored the word that the 'intensive' meaning grows.

Whether it occurs in isolation as here, or in a cluster as in Shakespeare or Shelley or Auden, or as a unit in a more or less pure image-vocabulary as in Pound or in the early Eliot or in Dylan Thomas, essentially, I think, a metaphor breaks up the literal meaning and shocks you into attending to the suggested meaning that accompanies or follows it. It is impossible to test this hypothesis on a bunch or series of metaphors and determine whether each metaphor delivers its separate shock and introduces its own complement of suggested meaning; or only contributes to the general dissolution of literalness and the creation of a climate of evocation; or does neither. It is obviously easier to study the behaviour of a metaphor when it is isolated in an environment of literal statement. An isolated metaphor will then be found disrupting not only the literalness of the statement which holds it but also the pervasive literalness of the passage where the statement occurs. The first disruption is the metaphor's essential function. The second, though it obviously is no invariable component of a metaphor's action, contributes to the shock as surely as the first does.[17] (This phenomenon—the solitary metaphor—is the reverse of what Day Lewis describes at some length in *The Poetic Image*—a flow of images being arrested either by an explicit general statement which gets them into perspective or by a flat colloquial statement in the post-Symbolist manner which shocks by its abrupt lowering of the emotional intensity.)[18]

It is naturally in Wordsworth, in the later Eliot and in the later Milton that one looks for passages of bare statement where the lone metaphor can be seen at work. The first sixty lines of the Third Book of *The Prelude* are sustained statement, a Chaucerian description of the bustling Cambridge scene. Tasselled cap, powdered hair, silk hose, college kitchens and the Trinity clock are presented in plain or in periphrastic language, and the metaphors such as there are are of the unobtrusive faded variety. Suddenly the even surface of statement is broken as a great metaphor shoulders itself above it—the metaphor of Newton's mind

for ever
Voyaging through strange seas of Thought, alone.

There cannot be a more adequate symbol for the scientific imagination than the *voyageur* image, but there is more to the metaphor than what it in itself is or means. The incongruity—the mind behind immobile stone being a wanderer—which breaks up the literal meaning of the statement and the agitation it sets up in the prevailing plainness of discourse make us sense a purpose behind the poet's departure from statement here, and we become aware of the presence of peripheral meaning, the suggestion of a mystery which the passage that follows describes, however fumblingly: Wordsworth's mind, in solitude, turned first inward and then outward, pushing its search to the very edge of sanity, in an attempt to marry external forms to inward states. The anticipatory suggestion of this phenomenon is not generated but only triggered by the mariner metaphor. Even if the metaphor were not there, the words that precede it (Newton's 'silent face, / The marble index of a mind . . . ' seen 'by light / Of moon or favouring stars') would carry the latent meaning that to Wordsworth the secret workings which the silence and repose of marble belie are the workings of his own mind, not Newton's. But this meaning would have remained latent and unapprehended, but for the metaphor.

Clearly in this part of the Third Book, Wordsworth is struggling to express certain operations of the mind which elude description and can perhaps only be shadowed faintly. The Newton passage is followed by another spell (some thirty-odd lines) of discursive literalness whose sole *raison d'être* seems to be to let itself be shattered by a curiously striking metaphor—Wordsworth's mind, when he had detached himself from Cambridge's dazzling show, 'into herself returning' and then with 'prompt rebound' regaining freshness and spreading itself 'with a wider creeping'—an athlete's or a ball's feat of instantly successive or near-simultaneous action and reaction, performed by the mind, perhaps to get uncoupled from 'the crowd, buildings and groves' and direct itself toward ' . . . universal things . . . The common countenance of earth and sky'. The secret of this obscure operation—which must have been of some importance to Wordsworth, for he reverts to it twice in the next 110 lines—will let itself be spoken only through suggestion. Suggestion here is liberated by the recoil metaphor which, rising above a stretch of level matter-of-factness, introduces the athlete-(ball)-mind incongruity.

How Michael's spirit, reborn through his companionship with his ten-year-old son, survived the betrayal of that companionship is the central meaning of Wordsworth's *Michael*. But neither a neat propositional statement like this nor the narration and description in the passage which speaks of the rebirth can quite render the quality of that experience. The overtones of meaning which uniquely render it are set afloat by a double metaphor which introduces the uneasy marriage of percept and affect and violates the consistent literalness of the passage:

> . . . from the Boy there came
> Feelings and emanations—things which were
> Light to the sun and music to the wind.

T. S. Eliot's play, *The Elder Statesman*, has a similar theme —the redemption and regeneration of an old man through the love of his daughter. There is the line spoken by Lord Claverton:

> I have been brushed by the wing of happiness . . .

The impact of the metaphor is violent, for apart from the action of the bird image on the line itself (compare it with the earlier unmetaphorical half-line:' . . . And now I feel happy—'), the image bursts in at the end of a speech that, for all its charge of feeling, is sternly austere in language, its only two deviations from literalness being two metaphors which are worn so thin as to be hardly noticeable as metaphors. In fact, it bursts in at the end of a play whose whole tone and language, like those of its predecessors, are skilfully stepped down to the low voltage of normal conversation. The image defines the quality of the happiness Lord Claverton has found—sudden, descended from above, evanescent; but its more important office is to make us aware of the fuller import of this moment of self-renewal and its far-ranging significance in terms of the whole play, perhaps of the whole series of plays of which this is the last.

In *Samson Agonistes* the image (in its form a simile, not a metaphor) of the 'two massie pillars' as mountains, which tremble 'with the force of winds and waters pent', rears itself above the sustained plainness of the Messenger's curiously objective reporting. The point of the image is obvious enough, but occurring where it does, it lifts the meaning from the referential to the evocative plane and attunes our ears to the larger resonance of that climactic encounter of the irresistible and the apparently irremovable—a widening significance which takes us farther afield to Milton's own predicament.

A fifth and last instance. The opening lines of Robert Lowell's 'Memories of West Street and Lepke', which record personal information in utterly unfigurative, almost sterilized language, end by suddenly erupting into metaphor:

> Like the sun she rises in her flame-flamingo infants' wear.

The immediate action of the triple metaphor is to specify the colour of the garment, but it would be strange if that were all when three vehicles—sun, flame and flamingo, all equally at odds with a nine-month-old child—are massed in a single line. They make a dry narration of facts end by exploding into centrifugal meaning. The image for red reaches out to the world, as yet unrevealed at this point, of disintegration and despair which the succeeding parts of the poem chart.

Not all metaphors, of course, work quite this way. All that is claimed here is that often (if not always, as Sanskrit poetics insists) a metaphor carries a load of suggestion and that in certain conditions its momentary disruption of logical discourse quickens the reader's sense of the suggested meaning. This last happens only when the nature and the situation of a metaphor permit it, but when it does happen, it is a noteworthy effect—striking in itself and perhaps significant also as an exploded model of a metaphor, showing—something which we would otherwise not be able to observe—how a metaphor essentially works.

6

Stating and Suggesting by Turns

What makes a poem switch from image to discourse or from discourse to image? One of the major achievements of recent critical theory has been to qualify the assumed polarity between the intensive manifold principle and the moral discourse principle and to recognize that symbol can be taught to lie down with discourse. Yet suggestion and statement giving rise to two opposed kinds of poem—Blake's 'Echoing Green' and Goldsmith's 'Deserted Village', to use Tillyard's examples[1]—is an old concept; as old in fact as ninth-century Sanskrit poetics which distinguished between *dhvanikāvya* (suggestive poetry) and *citrakāvya* (representational poetry); and it is a concept that apparently still rules our thinking so that we mostly have either studies of symbolist poetry or studies, like Donald Davie's,[2] of 'the poetry of urbane statement'. We do not seem to recognize that qualitative and rational progression as alternating modes within the same poem can be as significant a feature as the exclusive use of either. In fact, the alternation process can perhaps reveal better, because it does this contrastively, the cause and nature of either mode.

If poetry is not rhetoric, it cannot be all vision either; various *a priori* reasons have been assigned to show why it cannot. In the first place, poetry is words—and an art which employs verbal forms cannot altogether avoid discourse. The Symbolist aesthetic never looked this basic linguistic problem in the face. In the second place, although the extreme theoretical position is that by image is meant not this or that bit in a poem but the poem itself, yet most of us will agree that revelation through symbol is, by its very nature, intermittent and exists as high moments linked by a process of social syntactic narration which acts, to use Pound's phrase, as 'binding matter'. But these, I am afraid, are merely general explanations of why a poem is necessarily an articulation of symbolic and discursive components. It would be more useful perhaps to take a few very familiar poems—mostly anthology pieces—and note why there is in each a transition from the one principle to the other.

> Now it is fog, I walk
> Contained within my coat;
> No castle more cut off
> By reason of its moat:
> Only the sentry's cough,
> The mercenaries' talk.
>
> The street lamps, visible,
> Drop no light on the ground,
> But press beams painfully
> In a yard of fog around.
> I am condemned to be
> An individual.
>
> In the established border
> There balances a mere
> Pinpoint of consciousness.
> I stay, or start from, here:
> No fog makes more or less
> The neighbouring disorder.
>   (Thom Gunn, 'Human Condition')

G

The first two stanzas are mythopoeic, but at the end of the second, Gunn has already started explicating the import of the myth. Having presented the vehicle of the metaphor —the man in the coat walking through the fog—Gunn will not let it do its work by itself; he must go on to state the tenor. This probably means a gain in lucidity, but to know what has meantime been lost, one has only to turn to Gunn's poem 'Round and Round' which has the same theme, existential isolation. 'Round and Round' shows the interior of a lighthouse where the keeper has assembled his minimum essentials—'A wife, a wireless, bread and brains' —and these dance round with their faces turned toward the centre. Nothing more is said. The manner of 'Human Condition' recalls the explicitness of pre-Symbolist poetry and is a conscious reaction against the tenor-muffling which the Symbolist tradition used as a tool of suggestion. The Symbolist symbol is the self-sufficient vehicle pointing to an unnamed tenor; on the other hand in poetry such as that of Wordsworth, Shelley, Tennyson or Arnold we occasionally encounter moments when the myth having been presented, the meaning is taken up for unfolding. What invariably results is inanition of the image.

The effect is much the same or even worse when, as happens in the following passages, the sequence is reversed and the tenor is first offered, then the vehicle. Both passages present the hermit image, which is no more than a coincidence; both—and this is the point—preface it with a generalization.

> Soul and body have no bounds:
> To lovers as they lie upon
> Her tolerant enchanted slope
> In their ordinary swoon,

Grave the vision Venus sends
Of supernatural sympathy,
Universal love and hope;
While an abstract insight wakes
Among the glaciers and the rocks
The hermit's sensual ecstasy.
       (Auden, 'Lay your Sleeping Head, my Love')

Civilisation is hooped together, brought
Under a rule, under the semblance of peace
By manifold illusion; but man's life is thought,
And he, despite his terror, cannot cease
Ravening through century after century,
Ravening, raging, and uprooting that he may come
Into the desolation of reality:
Egypt and Greece, goodbye, and good-bye, Rome!
Hermits upon Mount Meru or Everest,
Caverned in night under the drifted snow,
Or where that snow and winter's dreadful blast
Beat down upon their naked bodies, know
That day brings round the night, that before dawn
His glory and his monuments are gone.
                        (Yeats, 'Meru')

The anticipatory affirmation that both these passages start
with does greater damage to the image than a tenor-naming
afterpiece could. Instead of thought and image getting formed
together, the thought is pre-existent, and the image, however potent in itself, merely illustrates a proffered idea ex-
traneously and is thus depressed to the level of a trope. This
can be seen happening in another poem of Auden's:

About suffering they were never wrong,
The Old Masters: how well they understood
Its human position; how it takes place

> While someone else is eating or opening a window
>   or just walking dully along;
> How, when the aged are reverently, passionately
>   waiting
> For the miraculous birth, there always must be
> Children who did not specially want it to happen,
>   skating
> On a pond at the edge of the wood . . .
>
> ('Musée des Beaux Arts')

Eliot has a similar image of the world's unconcern and
normalcy on the day of Nativity, a strangely similar image
because Eliot too calls the birth 'hard and bitter agony',
though in a different sense:

> Then we came to a tavern with vine-leaves over the lintel,
> Six hands at an open door dicing for pieces of silver,
> And feet kicking the empty wine-skins.
> But there was no information, and so we continued . . .
>
> ('Journey of the Magi')

Eliot's image, with no prefatory exposition to impoverish it,
is free-standing and vital.

Where what is suggested is also stated, the suggested
meaning (as we saw in Chapter 4) loses its paramountcy and
what we then have is not suggestive poetry but 'the poetry
of subordinate suggestion' (*guṇībhūtavyaṅgya*). Whether the
tenor is expounded before presenting the vehicle or after,
the effect is to debilitate the image; Sanskrit critics would
have no difficulty in classifying as *guṇībhūtavyaṅgya* the
passages from Gunn, Yeats and Auden that we have examined. However, since each of these passages only expresses
the same thing twice over, stating and suggesting it by turns,
I am afraid they do not represent the process this chapter is

centrally concerned with, which is the process of shifting
from the suggestive to the discursive mode or the other way
round, *in response to a shift in content*. An example of this
process is found in Yeats's 'Two Songs from a Play':

> In pity for man's darkening thought
> He walked that room and issued thence
> In Galilean turbulence;
> The Babylonian starlight brought
> A fabulous, formless darkness in;
> Odour of blood when Christ was slain
> Made all Platonic tolerance vain
> And vain all Doric discipline.
>
> Everything that man esteems
> Endures a moment or a day . . .

The whole of the first song and the first stanza, quoted
here, of the second song are propelled by a series of symbols
which, however pregnant and luminous, make no con-
cessions to the intellect. At the end of the intense sequence
we arrive at the direct assertion which the second stanza
opens with: 'Everything that man esteems Endures a moment or a day.' The metaphors that follow—the painter's
brush, the herald's cry, the soldier's tread—are so well-worn
as to be almost flush with the level of literal vocabulary;
they blend easily with the conceptualized nature of the
statement they support. The psychological rationale of this
transition to discourse is obvious. The discrete iridescent
symbols were a series of rapids and the stream must now
debouch into the commonalty and comprehensibility of a
generalization and subside to a sedate pace. Something like
this is what Cecil Day Lewis talks about in the passage I
referred to in the last chapter, where he calls the discursive

pause 'a point of vantage where we may rest a moment, review the image-sequence over which we have passed, and grasp its significance'.[3]

The device in Yeats's 'Two Songs' is, of course, different from the built-in paraphrase I illustrated from Gunn. The statement beginning 'Everything that man esteems . . . ' is not an explication of the import of the symbols; it is an independent statement, arising from, but not re-expressing, what the symbols intimate. The symbol-sequence was a vision of the two great cycles of history; in the last stanza the poem turns aside from this to affirm that each of man's achievements perishes but not until it has used up something of him that has gone into it.

Reverse the 'Two Songs' method, and you get a formula whereby a spell of matter of fact is arrested by an abrupt heightening. The even tenor of a flat description, narration or piece of reasoning is broken when the voltage un-expectedly rises, and a resonant moment arrives which draws its power from the very stretch of referential exposi-tion it helped to end. Masters of the literal, like Frost, are equally masters of this effect. The first three stanzas, for instance, of his 'Stopping by Woods on a Snowy Evening' are a straightforward account of the woods, the evening and the horse. The poem then instantly flowers into the evocativeness of the last stanza which obviously owes its force to the literalness of what went before.

The two passages from Yeats that we examined yield two different explanations for a poem exchanging abstraction for concretion or *vice versa*. Interestingly enough, there is a third explanation available, again from Yeats, from the Byzantium poems. John Bayley makes the point that the use of self-contained symbols with 'a conversational *armature*

in between' (as in 'Sailing to Byzantium') is Yeats's solution
for the Symbolist difficulty that an elaborate and unified
structure of symbols (as in 'Byzantium') tends to develop
allegorical reference.[4] Further explanations for sandwiching
statement between symbols can be had, I think, from T. S.
Eliot's poetry and criticism.

Eliot's development after *Ash Wednesday* was away from
pure suggestion and towards the interleaving of suggestion
with statement. *Four Quartets*, which represents the consummation of this process, is an elaborate essay in oscilla-
tion between image and discourse.

> There is no end of it, the voiceless wailing,
> No end to the withering of withered flowers,
> To the movement of pain that is painless and motionless,
> To the drift of the sea and the drifting wreckage,
> The bone's prayer to Death its God. Only the hardly,
>   barely prayable
> Prayer of the one Annunciation.
>
> It seems, as one becomes older,
> That the past has another pattern, and ceases to be a mere
>   sequence—
> Or even development: the latter a partial fallacy
> Encouraged by superficial notions of evolution,
> Which becomes, in the popular mind, a means of
>   disowning the past.
>
> ('The Dry Salvages')

This is typical of the way the non-discursive and discursive
modes succeed each other in *Four Quartets*, and for an explanation of why any poem should be founded on such
alternation we can turn to Eliot himself—to his criticism.
Didn't he say, ' . . . the poet, at the back of his mind, if not
as his ostensible purpose, is always trying to defend the

kind of poetry he is writing, or to formulate the kind that he wants to write . . . '?[5] The date of 'The Dry Salvages' is 1941. In the Ker Memorial lecture he gave in 1942, Eliot is found trying to defend the kind of poetry he was writing or to formulate the kind that he wanted to write. He argues that 'in a poem of any length, there must be transitions between passages of greater and less intensity', and that 'this test of the greatness of a poet is the way he writes his less intense, but structurally vital, matter'.[6] As Poe saw, texture implies brevity; conversely, length implies structure, and by 1942 Eliot had travelled all the way from pure texture to texture worked into structure. The *Quartets* are elaborately structured, with the 'less intense matter' and suggestive writing deployed in a well-defined pattern that repeats itself in each poem. Eliot's 'less intense matter' is, of course, the same concept as Pound's 'binding matter' and John Bayley's 'intellectual armature'.

A second reason Eliot produces elsewhere for the to-and-fro movement between the prosaic and the poetic is that length implies variety and variety implies smoothness of such movement. 'It is indeed necessary for any long poem, if it is to escape monotony, to be able to say homely things without bathos, as well as to take the highest flights without sounding exaggerated.'[7] This is true enough, but Eliot has a third and strikingly perspicacious explanation for the image-discourse alternation. The transitions, he says, 'give a rhythm of fluctuating emotion essential to the musical structure of the whole'.[8] This extremely significant concept is developed fully in his lecture, 'Poetry and Drama', where he demonstrates how the change from mere verse to poetry and back in the opening scene of *Hamlet* yields a musical pattern that alternately 'checks and accelerates the pulse of our emotion'.[9]

This can happen, as he points out, twice in the space of four lines:

> So have I heard, and do in part believe it.
> But, look, the morn, in russet mantle clad,
> Walks o'er the dew of yon high eastern hill.
> Break we our watch up.

Of course, the disposition of statement and suggestion is a vastly more intricate business in poetic drama where, as Eliot points out, the musical design should parallel the dramatic structure and a given utterance should express either character (where it does not meaningfully transcend it) or situation. In non-dramatic poetry, where these complicating factors are absent, the musical design tends simply to reproduce the archetypal pattern of repose and excitement.

Apart from the analogy of music, I think the fact that emotion, by its very nature, continually ceases and reappears dictates the dialectic of discourse and image. The transition from ebb to flow of emotion is accompanied by a transition from statement to suggestion (or the other way round, as the case may be), because emotion does not tolerate discourse. Frost's 'Birches' is a useful model demonstrating this process. There is first a bare description of the way the boy climbs the birches and alights from the swinging branches; apart from the point made that the game flatters the boy's sense of mastery, the account is free of all tinge of emotion. The line

> So was I once myself a swinger of birches

signals a sharp change in direction and interest. The poet swings round from the boy to himself, from fact to feeling, from the denotative to the connotative manipulation of language—and the boy's birch-swinging which was an objectively recorded game continues as his own birch-swinging, an image now, suggestive of the mutual tension within him of the escapist and homing emotions.

7

Statement Poetry

Is there such a thing as statement poetry at all? When Tillyard says, 'All poetry is more or less oblique: there is no direct poetry',[1] or when Wimsatt says, 'Poetry is never altogether, or even mainly, "poetry of statement" ',[2] if all they mean is that there is an element of suggestion in the most pedestrian discursive poem (even as there is an alloy of discourse in the most intensely symbolist poetry), that is something one would have no difficulty in granting, since it cannot be claimed for either kind of poetry, or indeed for any kind, that it occurs in a pure state. We talk about 'statement poetry' only because the difference between Cowper's *The Task* and Mallarmé's *L'Après-midi d'un Faune* is so great that we cannot pretend that they are the same kind of writing.

But it was on altogether different grounds from these that the existence of statement poetry was denied by Susanne Langer. If by statement poetry, she says, is meant poetry which offers direct propositions, then it is not poetry at all, as propositions belong to science and are alien to art. Now this is largely a matter of how you choose to define 'poetry'; a definition which excluded Chaucer and Dryden and several parts of Wordsworth would not have much to recommend it. Mrs Langer does not indeed exclude them—her manner of attacking statement in poetry is to engulf it (as the amoeba engulfs its prey) and assimilate it into her theory. According to this theory of art as symbolic form, when a poet states a thought directly, his stating of it is an illusion and what has really happened is that the thinking of that thought—an occurrence in the thinker's personal history, an experience lived and felt by him—has got presented. But this is something Lascelles Abercrombie had said twenty-seven years before Susanne Langer. Speaking of the 'Time hath, my Lord, a wallet' speech in *Troilus and Cressida*, he says the real matter of the passage is not the thought it presents, 'because it is not presented to us simply as *thought*, but as the finely emotional and subtly allusive experience of an individual mind *thinking*—of, precisely, Shakespeare's Ulysses thinking'.[3] There is, no doubt, something in this, but a theory which assumes that every stated thought in poetry is a semblance beneath which is the reality—the process of thinking and feeling—frustrates itself by its very inclusiveness. By this token, for instance, instead of identifying the following lines as pedestrian verse offering a mere proposition about human treachery, we would have to salute them as symbolizing the poet Rochester's entertainment of the thought. The point about the lines, of course, is that underneath the deadening abstraction, the experience, if there is any, has so feeble a pulse:

> Which is the basest *Creature*, *Man* or *Beast*?
> *Birds* feed on *Birds*, *Beasts* on each other prey,
> But Savage *Man* alone, does *Man* betray:
> Prest by necessity, they Kill for Food,
> *Man* undoes *Man*, to do himself no good.
>
> ('A Satyr against Mankind')

But we ought not really to be talking about individual lines and passages when our concern in this chapter is with *whole* poems. We are dealing here with statement poetry as a *genre*, and neither with statement as a mode alternating with the suggestive mode within a poem (see the last chapter) nor with statement—stated meaning, that is—as a component of meaning, serving as a base for the other component, i.e. suggested meaning (see Chapter 4). Statement poetry—poems that are merely expository, descriptive or narrative—has a long history and is still a living form—it is an unbroken tradition stretching from Gower or farther back all the way down to Betjeman. Sanskrit criticism calls this *genre* 'representational or pictorial poetry' (*citrakāvya*), distinguishing it from 'suggestive poetry' (*dhvanikāvya*)* and from 'the poetry of subordinate suggestion' (*guṇībhūta-vyaṅgya*). The distinction between poetry where the suggested meaning is secondary and poetry where it is paramount is not easy to sustain—at any rate, not easy to demonstrate. But the notion that poetry aiming merely at representing or stating does exist can be a useful corrective to the heresy that statement in poetry is an illusion or a kind of prestidigitation.

Citrakāvya is a pejorative term—Sanskrit criticism regards statement poetry as an inferior, if not wholly illegitimate, kind. This, I think, is an equally useful concept. Donald Davie, whose expositions of statement poetry are the best available yet, concedes that to find 'purity of diction', which he equates with 'strength of statement', 'we should look not among our great poets but among our good ones'.[4] Susanne Langer, on the contrary, argues that the distinction between statement poetry and oblique poetry 'rests on a difference of technical means rather than of poetic excel-

* 'All Art that is not mere story-telling, or mere portraiture, is symbolic.' (Yeats, *Ideas of Good and Evil*)

lence',[5] and that since Blake's means and Goldsmith's means, although different, are means to the same end, the idea of a special standard to judge Goldsmith by is artificial. Of course, once we get outside the terms of Mrs Langer's theory of statement as semblance, we see easily enough that a value judgement is implicit in the very term 'statement poetry'. And this has never been clearer than today. Aside from interludes like the Movement, the commitment to indirection and semantic richness as essentials of the best poetry is almost universal in our age. However, our age is also known to have a weakness for description and analysis, at the expense of evaluation, in criticism, and there is always the danger that our perception of degrees of excellence will be deadened if the notion that the status of statement poetry is essentially different is not insisted upon.

On grounds very different from Mrs Langer's it can be made out that discursive and suggestive are not absolute categories and that whether a poem is suggestive or the opposite depends on how you read it. You could, if you tried hard enough, read Cowper as though he were Swinburne and Swinburne as though he were Cowper. This would no doubt be an exercise calling for an effort and feasible only within limits, but it *is* feasible, and I could try to establish its feasibility by means of a demonstration. But this has already been done for us. In *Interpretations*, the concluding four lines of 'Among School Children'—for range and richness of meaning, probably the most remarkable single passage in English poetry of this century—are treated by John Wain as merely referential and disposed of in the following brief paraphrase:

...the confused relationship of matter and spirit. Even blossoming and dancing are accompanied by this confusion; a chestnut-tree has a massive trunk, cool green leaves, and delicate blossoms; at which point is one most in touch with its essential identity? Again, a dancer is the embodiment of the dance; without the tangible, moving body, the dance would not exist; nevertheless it is a perceptible thing in itself. This question is brought up, but it is not the function of the poem to propound a solution . . .[6]

In the very next chapter, G. S. Fraser demonstrates how an immense wealth of meaning can be read into Denham's well-known four lines on the Thames which, their metaphors notwithstanding, are explicit and direct. Now Fraser, not Wain, typifies the reading habit of our time. Trained by contemporary writing to be perpetually tuned-in to unspoken meanings, the twentieth-century reader tends to respond to 'The Deserted Village' or even 'An Essay on Criticism' in this way. This does work—but not all the time and not beyond a point, because a successful poem makes you read it the way it wants to be read and effectively rejects any other way as alien to its nature. In other words, you cannot, except as a *tour de force*, read Cowper as though he were Swinburne nor Swinburne as though he were Cowper.

The case for conceding that statement poetry can exist in its own right is, I think, strong. It has, in fact, so existed since Chaucer or as far back as one cares to push—and as an unbroken tradition, central and prestigious during certain periods and tending to withdraw to the periphery during others. Indeed a whole poem structured on narration, description or exposition and employing lucid, image-free, self-contained statement as its language has been such a familiar form in the past that it is unnecessary to offer examples, although some poets have been more closely identified with this mode than others, and one thinks here of Chaucer, Gower, Dryden, Pope, Johnson, Goldsmith, Cowper, Crabbe and Clare. The list stops short of our own century—and so it would even if it were more detailed and comprehensive. Today a long discursive poem, when one does get written, is a distinguished exception.

While talking thus about the fortunes of statement poetry, one has got to be very wary of the occupational hazards of literary history so impressively illustrated in the fate of Eliot's theory of how discourse and image (or thought and feeling, if you like) got dissociated in 1650 or thereabouts. It is not arbitrary, I think, to take it that Edgar Allan Poe's attack (in *The Poetic Principle*) on the idea of the long poem was the starting point, or at least was the first sign, of the decline of statement poetry. The attack was motivated by the premises of the aesthetic he was enunciating; his theory of suggestiveness could be erected only on the dead body of the long poem, because (although a few long poems in the Symbolist mode have indeed been achieved) intensity presupposes brevity. Poe's objections to statement and to length were soon refined and developed into the central assumptions of the Symbolist poetic. But quite apart from Poe and the Symbolists, the popularity of Palgrave's *Golden Treasury* (1861/69) was creating a taste for the intense short-flighted lyric, and the novel was fast replacing the long narrative poem as fireside family reading. In the manifestos of the first wave of the 'revolution', Mallarmé, building on Schopenhauer's ideas, had defined the change as the replacing of the language of naming and description with the language of suggestion; in the manifestos of the second wave, Hulme, building on Bergson's ideas, defined the change as the replacing of language 'as an abstract process' with the language of images serving as 'a compromise for a language of intuition'.[7] This movement away from directness and explicitness and indeed from logical and social values has ruled out the use of statement as a poem's normal voice and demoted it to a secondary rôle either as coarse connective tissue or as an alternative mode to switch to occasionally. Further, in our own times, texture in poetry and close reading in criticism have concurrently grown in importance. It is difficult to decide which of the two is the cause and which the effect, but both the trends have clearly worked against the extended use of statement in poetry.

Nevertheless, statement poetry still persists although as a somewhat isolated tradition, and an examination of a few samples of this surviving mode will probably turn out to be a better aid to an understanding of its decline than my timid excursion into literary history has been. Also, the differentia and rationale of statement poetry are more easily discernible in its present-day models than in earlier ones, because it is not the normal kind today and its features acquire greater definition against the reigning mode.

A work that can serve as a point of departure for this enquiry is Robert Lowell's *Life Studies*—not the whole volume, but the third part, forming a separate sequence of poems, after which the book itself is named. *Life Studies* has been described as a breakthrough in Lowell's work in several ways, but what is most strikingly novel in it is the laconic featureless language of case-histories in which it records events in Lowell's own life and in the lives of other Lowells and Winslows. If his well-known early poem 'The Quaker Graveyard in Nantucket' is stylistically his *Paradise Lost* (the comparison is Randall Jarrell's), then *Life Studies* can well be his *Paradise Regained*, representing a movement

H

away from verbal richness and indirection and toward austere bareness of statement. 'The Quaker Graveyard' speaks of Warren Winslow's death thus:

> The wind's wings beat upon the stones,
> Cousin, and scream for you and the claws rush
> At the sea's throat and wring it in the slush
> Of this old Quaker graveyard where the bones
> Cry out in the long night for the hurt beast
> Bobbing by Ahab's whaleboats in the East.

In the late 'forties, when Lowell mourned the death of his grandfather, Arthur Winslow, it was still in the same language:

>   and the ghost
> Of risen Jesus walks the waves to run
> Arthur upon a trumpeting black swan
> Beyond Charles River to the Acheron
> Where the wide waters and their voyager are one.
>   ('In Memory of A. W.')

The congestion of imagery here, the coiling eloquence, the myths from antiquity, religion and literature and the incantatory phraseology and rhythm raise the language of these passages to an extraordinary degree of complication and intensity of meaning. *Life Studies*, on the other hand, exhibits the terminal result of the process of dilution and sterilization to which Lowell subjected his language in order to reduce it to transparent referential statement. Lowell's passages on death in *Life Studies*—first his father's death and then his mother's—are a strange contrast to the early elegiac moments:

Father's death was abrupt and unprotesting.
His vision was still twenty-twenty.
After a morning of anxious, repetitive smiling,
his last words to Mother were:
'I feel awful.'

       ('Terminal Days at Beverly Farms')

Mother travelled first-class in the hold,
her Risorgimento black and gold casket
was like Napoleon's at the *Invalides* . . .

In the grandiloquent lettering on Mother's coffin,
Lowell had been misspelled *LOVEL.*
The corpse
was wrapped like *panetone* in Italian tinfoil.

       ('Sailing home from Rapallo')

  The language of *Life Studies* is dead-pan matter-of-fact reporting, relieved by a very occasional heightening; and the
bleakness of the language is matched by the muted verse.
'To a Cisalantic ear', says F. W. Bateson, 'they [the *Life
Studies* poems] are rhythmically formless, prose disguised as
verse by chopping it up into short lines.'[8]

Given a year,
I walked on the roof of the West Street Jail, a short
enclosure like my school soccer court,
and saw the Hudson River once a day
through sooty clothesline entanglements
and bleaching khaki tenements.
Strolling, I yammered metaphysics with Abramowitz,
a jaundice-yellow ('it's really tan')
and fly-weight pacifist,
so vegetarian,
he wore rope shoes and preferred fallen fruit.

> He tried to convert Bioff and Brown,
> the Hollywood pimps, to his diet.
> Hairy, muscular, suburban,
> wearing chocolate double-breasted suits,
> they blew their tops and beat him black and blue.
> ('Memories of West Street and Lepke')

This reads like the transcript of a recording of casual coffee-bar reminiscing; but the shame and despair within, the corruption and disruption of the psyche, wait in the background, and the lines have a menacing aspect. This does not, however, alter the fact that the style represents an experiment in drastic paring down to starkly simple statement. The unique idiom of *Life Studies* stands out the more sharply because Lowell's more recent work—*Near the Ocean* (1967), for instance—represents a return to symbol-making and to tighter and more obvious rhythms. The concluding stanza of 'Fourth of July in Maine' is typical:

> We watch the logs fall. Fire once gone,
> we're done for: we escape the sun,
> rising and setting, a red coal,
> until it cinders like the soul.
> Great ash and sun of freedom, give
> us this day the warmth to live,
> and face the household fire. We turn
> our backs, and feel the whiskey burn.

The *raison d'être* of Lowell's excursion into statement poetry is, I think, clear enough. His evolution up to the point represented by *Life Studies* was from bardic intensity to dramatic speech and thence to confessional sincerity; and obeying the logic of this development, his language changed from image and incantation to the variety and ease of the

speaking voice and then to plain statement. Now the 'I' of
the dramatic monologue denotes only its protagonist and if
it ever has any relation to the poet, it is to the poet with the
'mask' on. This 'I' is, therefore, a franchise for the imaginary
in content and the imaginative in style. On the other hand,
the 'I' of the avowedly confessional poem stands, quite
literally, for the person who wrote it and commits him to
accurate presentation of autobiographical fact and, equally,
to a language appropriate to unrefracted transmission of information. To state this distinction in even simpler terms,
the poetic symbol and the confessional first person singular
are opposed principles—the former involves suggestiveness,
the latter involves statement. Of course, artistic sincerity
is more than literal veracity; artistic presentation of autobiographical material obviously does involve selection and
re-ordering with a view not merely to form but indeed to
the total truth. And the confessional 'I' can in certain cases
admit mythopoeia as, for instance, in the confession of
mystic experience; it can, I suppose, even admit self-
dramatizing to some extent. All the same, it would be, by
and large, right to say that symbol and ambiguity are the
language of essentially dramatic poetry like Eliot's and are
alien to the purposes of a confessional poet like the Lowell
of *Life Studies*. The *Life Studies* poems were originally accompanied, in the same volume, by a prose autobiographical
sketch, '91 Revere Street', whose content they largely echo.
If Lowell wanted to project in material form the concomitance of confession and prosaic statement, he couldn't have
used a better method.

The assumption I have offered of the concomitance of the
two has, of course, got to be tested on other samples of
confessional poetry. The most obvious sample from modern

poetry would be D. H. Lawrence's work, the poems which he classifies as 'personal' as distinguished from 'fictional'.[9] In his 'personal' poetry, of which the most impressive single body is the sequence, *Look! We have Come through!*, Lawrence discards the mask—or (to use his own metaphor) doesn't put his hand over the mouth of the demon in him and speak for him but lets him say his say.[10] Lawrence not only describes this sequence as personal but insists unequivocally that it should be treated as a factual autobiographical record of the years 1912 to 1917 in his life:

Even the best poetry, when it is at all personal, needs the penumbra of its own time and place and circumstance to make it full and whole. If we knew a little more of Shakespeare's self and circumstance how much more complete the Sonnets would be to us, how their strange, torn edges would be softened and merged into a whole body! So one would like to ask the reader of *Look! We have Come through!* to fill in the background of the poems, as far as possible, with the place, the time, the circumstance. What was uttered in the cruel spring of 1917 should not be dislocated and heard as if sounding out of the void.[11]

Here the objection in present-day criticism to the maskless poet inside the poem being identified with the man who wrote it is anticipated and effectively disarmed. Besides this, in *Look! We have Come through!* Lawrence is already using free verse, claiming for it that it 'is, or should be, direct utterance from the instant, whole man', utterance that 'rushes out without artificial foam or artificial smoothness'.[12] In a different context and on a different ground, Lawrence describes 'stark, bare, rocky directness of statement' as the essence of poetry today.[13]

Yet, for all these indications to the contrary, confession in direct language is precisely what *Look! We have Come through!* is not. By 'direct statement' Lawrence doesn't seem to have meant a transparent unfigurative style, a language reduced to the consistency of prose. Rather, the 'directness' he preaches denotes immediacy (as opposed to finish) in utterance, the pulsating plasm as opposed to the perfected unageing gem. This 'momentaneity' is the presiding principle of *Look! We have Come through!* Lawrence, of course, did practise stark, bare, rocky statement, but as the vehicle not of confession but of lively exact description, so that it is frequently encountered in the collection, *Birds, Beasts, and Flowers*:

> She is large and matronly
> And rather dirty,
> A little sardonic-looking, as if domesticity had driven
>   her to it.
> ·Though what she does, except lay four eggs at random
>   in the garden once a year
> and put up with her husband,
> I don't know.
>
> She likes to eat.
> She hurries up, striding reared on long uncanny legs
> When food is going.
> Oh yes, she can make haste when she likes.
>
> ('Lui et Elle')

This language of naturalistic portraiture is a far cry from the charged language of metaphor and resonance to which Lawrence was roused in the confessional passages of *Look! We have Come through!*:

> Then the sweeping sunshine of noon
> When the mountains like chariot cars
> Were ranked to blue battle—and you and I
> Counted our scars.

> And then in a strange, grey hour
> We lay mouth to mouth, with your face
> Under mine like a star on the lake,
> And I covered the earth, and all space.

('History')

Look! We have Come through! is an extended epithalamium shot with direct self-revelation, but it certainly does not employ the unechoing explicatory language of statement poetry.

John Betjeman's *Summoned by Bells*, which appeared a year after *Life Studies*, is also a full-length exercise in confessional statement poetry, but both its confession and its statement are noticeably different. *Look! We have Come through!* is, in Lawrence's words, 'a biography of an emotional and inner life',[14] and so is *Life Studies*. Confession, if that is the word, in *Summoned by Bells* is not a voice from the buried cellars of being—it moves, in the wake of Betjeman's bicycle, at the open-to-the-skies, sun-drenched level of 'those winding lanes of meadowsweet and umbelliferae'. Betjeman, who tells how he in his youth began in gladness, cannot ever claim that thereof came in the end despondency and madness. The sensibility he reveals is sophisticated but never demonic or tortured. His mode of statement too is different. Unlike Lowell's clipped taut sentences, Betjeman's are full and flowing; they are overt, explicit, completed, lucid—almost overpoweringly lucid.

It cannot be claimed that the discursiveness of *Summoned by Bells* was dictated by its confessional nature—discursiveness is Betjeman's native mode anyway. As Philip Larkin said, for Betjeman 'there has been no symbolism, no objective correlative, no T. S. Eliot or Ezra Pound, no rediscovery of myth or language as gesture, no *Seven Types* or *Some Versions*'.[15] A very brief analysis here of how all

Betjeman's instincts combine to make easy urbane discourse his inevitable medium might help in isolating the major determinants of statement poetry in general. To begin with, for Betjeman, communication is the first imperative; and the kind of *rapport* with the reader which his art demands as the very condition of its being establishes itself not at the subliminal level at which suggestion largely works but at the level of rational consecutive exposition. That places him firmly in the traditional line of present-day poets—and this in fact is the second determinant of statement poetry operative in Betjeman's case. What drew him to the 'Tooled leather, marbled paper, gilded edge' of old books and the lonely, heavily restored St Ervan's church in a Cornwall hollow must have also drawn him to traditional modes of poetic utterance with their emphasis on unfoldedness and socialness. Thirdly, Betjeman's devotion to the lineaments of the external landscape—manors and churches, 'lanes in beechy Bucks', Wiltshire cottages, the 'neo-Tudor shops' of suburbia, Cornwall beaches, and human beings ranging from Sarah the maid ('with orange wig and horsy teeth') to Maurice Bowra himself—gives his writing a strong bias toward down-to-earth description of an almost Chaucerian liveliness and gusto; and statement is its tool. And in Betjeman's case, the common disease of statement poetry, bathos, is averted by the prophylactic action of the mock-heroic vein and the readiness to laugh at himself.

Apart from illuminating thus some of the primary determinants of statement poetry, *Summoned by Bells* raises a question which, I think, is central to any examination of statement and suggestion. The prefatory note to the poem describes Betjeman as having gone 'as near prose as he dare'. Indeed, the poem is an exercise in brinkmanship of con-

siderable virtuosity, but Betjeman several times treads the
edge too confidently and is pitched into prose:

> Those were the days when Huxley's *Antic Hay*
> Shocked our conventions, when from month to month
> I rushed to buy *The London Mercury*,
> And moved from Austin Dobson on to Pope.

This is iambic prose and hasn't even got the light-verse
effect which redeems the Homeric catalogue of second-hand
books elsewhere in the poem:

> Mason's *Works*
> (But volume II is missing), Young's *Night Thoughts*,
> Falconer's *Shipwreck* and *The Grave* by Blair,
> A row of Scott, for certain incomplete,
> And always somewhere Barber's *Isle of Wight*;
> The antiquarian works that no one reads—
> *Church Bells of Nottingham, Baptismal Fonts*
> ('Scarce, 2s. 6d., a few plates slightly foxed').

The question we would be tempted to ask on encounter-
ing this kind of 'poetry' has already been asked—by Betjeman
himself in the prefatory note: 'Why is this account of some
moments in the sheltered life of a middle-class youth not
written in prose?'

And why, we may ask, is T. S. Eliot's play *The Confidential
Clerk* not written in prose?

> EGGERSON. You will wish to obtain confirmation
> Of this interesting discovery, Mr. Kaghan,
> By putting your adoptive parents in touch
> With Mrs. Guzzard. It's for them to confirm
> That they took you, as a child, from Mrs. Guzzard,
> To whom, it seems, you had first been entrusted.

This language, although clearly not quite identical with that of Betjeman's memoirs, prompts the same question as his, and if Betjeman, having put the question, did not answer it explicitly, Eliot has explained at some length, chiefly from the dramatist's angle, how statement poetry differs from prose. But Eliot's conception of the rôle of statement in poetic drama is developed from his conception of the rôle of statement in poetry in general, and we must look at the latter first. It is set forth in the lecture on 'The Music of Poetry' where Eliot makes the point that in a long poem suggestion is necessarily confined to certain moments when the suggestiveness or what he calls the 'allusiveness which is in the nature of words' is activated and that the rest of the poem is less intense matter; the structure of the poem rests on the disposition of the richer among the poorer words. This is a familiar enough notion; what is significant is Eliot's further assumption that the poorer words, which account for the bulk of the poem, are so vital to its structure that the way the poet manages them is a test of his greatness. In fact 'it may be said that no poet can write a poem of amplitude unless he is a master of the prosaic'.[16] The chief aspect of this mastery is the ability 'to say homely things without bathos'—a complementary skill to that of taking 'the highest flights without sounding exaggerated'.[17] Eliot adds a diachronic gloss on this binary view of the language of poetry—literary history, as he sees it, patterns as an alternation of periods when the language of poetry develops in the direction of elaboration and complication, with periods when it returns to the supple rhythms and direct vocabulary of spoken everyday language and catches up with its changes; exaggeration of the former tendency makes suggestiveness artificial and of the latter makes statement pedestrian.

It was these general assumptions about statement poetry that Eliot applied to the problems of drama when in the late 'thirties he started experimenting in a new kind of play. Reacting both against high-faluting poetic drama and naturalistic prose drama, and discarding the language of his own first major play, he proceeded to fashion the kind of statement poetry for drama that is typified in the *Confidential Clerk* passage we noted above. The language of conventional poetic drama was, of course, repugnant to contemporary life which was the stuff of his plays from *The Family Reunion* onwards. Prose, on the other hand, was equally alien to his purposes—when moments of emotional intensity made poetry the only valid language, the transition from prose to poetry could jolt the present-day audience (which, unlike the Elizabethan, regards poetry as many degrees removed from language in life) out of that unawareness of the medium which is the first condition of dramatic response. Statement poetry seemed to be the answer. It was, for one thing, poetry 'with nothing poetic about it . . . poetry so transparent that we should not see the poetry, but that which we are meant to see through the poetry';[18] secondly, it would enable him 'to bring poetry into the world in which the audience lives and to which it returns when it leaves the theatre';[19] thirdly, statement poetry would be a medium 'in which everything can be said that has to be said'.[20] It is true that when Eliot spoke of a new medium based on a 'proper modern colloquial idiom' as he called it, he meant not only a language composed of the unfigurative, unevocative vocabulary of educated conversation but also a metric made up of the natural stresses of contemporary speech which could replace blank verse now grown remote from spoken English and somewhat stiff in the joints. We are in this chapter strictly concerned only with the first of these two components—what Raymond Williams, speaking of the dialogue in *The Cocktail Party*, calls 'statement, of a deliberate lucidity, and with the minimum of imagery and evocation'.[21] Yet it seems to me that the answer to Betjeman's question, Why is this not written in prose? lies in the results achieved by Eliot's dramatic verse which, while as a rule carefully stopping short of the poetical, accomplishes a variety of jobs that prose cannot attempt. The verse is so self-effacingly unobtrusive that we are not aware that it has gone to work on us—particularly in the theatre, where, unless we have read the play, we have no means of knowing whether we are listening to verse or prose. The impact on us of the high points of intensity in the plays does bear out Eliot's claim that the ascent to these is rendered smooth for the modern audience when the ground level is verse, not prose. Apart from this, any scene in the plays would show that features of rhythm, which even in the most speech-based and loose verse are more precise and clearly marked than they would be in prose, can be made to serve as a gesture of individuality, to mark a rise in tension, or to colour a variation in tone. In addition, the basic pattern of three stresses, which is audible all the time as a subdued undertone and, though not consciously attended to, is nevertheless something the ear learns to expect, can, when departed from, signal a shift in the situation or a turn in the argument. If nothing else, the unceasing muffled ticking of the three-stress line can insinuate, amid the medley of voices, a suggestion of unity. Verse, as Eliot claimed, is never 'merely a formalization, or an added decoration',[22] and the potentialities of low-voltage verse, which Eliot's plays constantly worked towards realizing, can validate the

flattest statement poetry and give it an identity and status
distinct from those of prose.

> 'Your trouble is not sticking to the subject,'
> Pike said with temper. And Dick longed to say,
> 'Your trouble is bucolic lack of logic,'
> But all he did say was, ' What *is* the subject?'
> 'It's whether these professions really work.
> Now take the Doctor—'

In its directness, clarity and closeness to conversation, the
dialogue in Frost's 'From Plane to Plane' (the lines quoted
above are typical of the poem) shares the same language
with the dialogue in *The Confidential Clerk*. The language
of *The Confidential Clerk* we can easily enough recognize as
something Eliot voluntarily chose for a specific *genre*, but
in the case of Frost, there is the absurd phantom, not fully
exorcised yet, of the New England farmer who can do no
more than versify and naïvely moralize. For the dialogue in
'The Death of the Hired Man', Frost draws upon the same
plain language of everyday speech:

> 'No, but he hurt my heart the way he lay
> And rolled his old head on that sharp-edged chair-back.
> He wouldn't let me put him on the lounge.
> You must go in and see what you can do.
> I made the bed up for him there to-night.
> You'll be surprised at him—how much he's broken.
> His working days are done; I'm sure of it.'
>
> 'I'd not be in a hurry to say that.'
>
> 'I haven't been. Go, look, see for yourself.
> But, Warren, please remember how it is:
> He's come to help you ditch the meadow.
> He has a plan. You mustn't laugh at him . . . '

This is explicit narration of how Mary interceded with her husband for the human waif, Silas. But what this passage overtly states, an earlier passage in the poem has presented by image:

> Part of a moon was falling down the west,
> Dragging the whole sky with it to the hills.
> Its light poured softly in her lap. She saw
> And spread her apron to it. She put out her hand
> Among the harp-like morning-glory strings,
> Taut with the dew from garden bed to eaves,
> As if she played unheard some tenderness
> That wrought on him beside her in the night.

It is obvious from this that when Frost is not stating, he can wield the opposite method with equal assurance; but the point is that this is the poem's only passage in the language of image. Indeed, imagery is not, by any means, Frost's customary language. There are in fact two Frosts—a fact which both his critics and apologists seem to forget. Cleanth Brooks once said that 'Frost's themes are frequently stated overtly'[23] and that his best poetry, however, 'exhibits the structure of symbolist-metaphysical poetry'[24]—the distinction I am trying to draw here is different. There is, on the one hand, the Frost of 'Directive', 'Design', 'Acquainted with the Night', 'Sand Dunes', 'Come In' and like poems, who, whether his language be pregnant image or simple-seeming statement, is concerned to find a voice for his specifically twentieth-century sensibility, complex, in-growing and loneliness-haunted. There is then the other Frost who is content, through easily accessible verbal structures, to portray in realistic detail a scene, an animal, a human figure; or to develop a situation by coherent narration; or simply to present an unearned generalization. 'The Runaway', for instance, is a frankly naturalistic vignette of a young colt agitated by its first snow. 'Two Tramps in Mud-Time' paraphrasably affirms the wisdom of uniting love of work and need of work. 'From Plane to Plane' employs the sun not as a many-meaninged symbol but pointedly as a logical illustration of two concepts not poetically fully validated: the first, 'extrication' or detachment from professional activity; and the second, the donor's shyness of gratitude. 'The Death of the Hired Man' is an episode simply told and a somewhat Galsworthian portrait of failure; and, except for the very competent blank verse, it does not employ any device that would not be equally legitimate in a prose 'character' or short story. These poems are successful on their own plane, the plane of statement; to burden them with unstated significance and to despise, as some of Frost's apologists do, the reader who is content with their literal meaning is to thwart the proper response to them by forcing a reaction that is appropriate to a different kind of poem where Frost lets his inwardness speak either through symbol or through pregnant prosaic statement.

If we seek the origins of the discursive vein that distinguishes a great deal of Frost's work, we will find that although his statement poetry, at its plainest, subsists, in comparison with Betjeman's, at a different—or, if you like, higher—level, yet the same determinants of statement poetry are active in both. The compulsion to communicate successfully, to be, in the best sense of the word, popular, was strong in Frost. Secondly, his interest in places and persons, in seasons and creatures, in their real selves and for their individual sakes, was equally strong, so that a horse, a cow in Frost, unlike the members of Ted Hughes's menagerie, are a horse, a cow, neither more nor less. Thirdly, although

the idiom he fashioned for himself is a very individual instrument and its chattiness can at times be a cloak for less
obvious intimations, yet even while working toward effects
of this kind and certainly at other times, Frost is content to
operate within the framework of traditional modes of utterance and be discursive and intelligible. In fact, his commitment to economy of metaphor and allusion raises his
language to a higher degree of lucidity of affirmation than
one associates with traditional writing.

However, to equate unmetaphorical unallusive language
with statement, as we have sometimes done, is to over-
simplify, at least in certain cases. Pope's metaphors, for
instance, offer a univocal logical enunciation:

> For wit and judgment often are at strife,
> Tho' meant each other's aid, like man and wife.
> 'Tis more to guide, than spur the Muse's steed;
> Restrain his fury, than provoke his speed.
>
> ('An Essay on Criticism')

On the other hand, a poem like George MacBeth's well-
known 'Report to the Director' can affect the impersonal
colourlessness and workaday precision of civil service writing
or speech and yet, by its omissions and implications, develop
layers of sinister meaning:

> The infusion
> Was one of the smoothest I've seen. Evacuation
> Very decent. An infinity of freshness
> In a little diffusion of bitter carbolic. Rather sweet.
> It took about fifteen minutes to get the stories,
> And not much mess; they had to scrub the channel
> To clear some vomit, otherwise all O.K.

This kind of 'statement poetry' or understatement poetry,

I

beneath its carefully preserved discursive exterior, attempts suggestion without using the more familiar tools of suggestion like image, evocation or ellipsis. Much of the work of the Movement poets too, despite their professed contempt for 'the myth-kitty' and for incantation, and despite their definition of a poem as a structure of events or arguments, is sophisticated non-statement of this sort, fraught with a quantity of suggested meaning.

8

Suggestion as a Classical Method

'It is an obvious truth of romantic poetry', says John Bayley
in *The Romantic Survival*, 'that exact words usually "suggest" far more powerfully than vague ones.'[1] To be fair
to Mr Bayley, he makes this observation while examining
certain words in Dylan Thomas's poetry, which do manage
to be both exact and suggestive; and Dylan Thomas is
clearly a neo-romantic. Yet if I were generalizing, I would
be inclined to say the very opposite: that it is an obvious
truth of Romantic poetry that vague words usually suggest
far more powerfully than exact ones. It is the strength of
much Romantic poetry that, to borrow Wimsatt's words,
the 'shadowy suggestion of abstractive categorizing' forbids
us to descend to 'the substantive level'.[2] Shelley's 'Champak
odours', the nineteenth-century Thomson's 'wine of love'
and Swinburne's 'Grief with a glass that ran'[3] are typical
Romantic words; light in referential content, they float high
above the specifically qualificative plane. They are merely
centres of semantic radiation. Of course, all Romantics are
not alike. As T. S. Eliot says, 'The bird of Wordsworth
"breaking the silence of the seas" remains; the swallow of
"Itylus" disappears'.[4] Wordsworth's cuckoo does refer to the
object, while Swinburne's swallow is little more than the
word's sound and associations.

Yet the difference is only one of degree; and if Swinburne's swallow differs qualitatively from any bird, it is from Eliot's own plover. The bent golden-rod and the whirling plover of *Ash Wednesday* are, in the first place, solidly denotative and form an exact notation of the New England coastal scene. In the second place, their suggestiveness is not unlimited but points firmly to a specific inward experience. The difference is seen no less in the use of less visually concrete images. The time symbol, for instance, works in radically different ways in the following two passages:

> Before the beginning of years
>   There came to the making of man
> Time with a gift of tears;
>   Grief with a glass that ran . . .
>
> (Swinburne)

> Time and the bell have buried the day,
> The black cloud carries the sun away.
> Will the sunflower turn to us . . .
>
> (Eliot)

Eliot's, I think, is an experiment which, though half a century old now, is still of great interest and significance. It also links itself, across the intervening centuries and despite great differences, with another experiment.

Suggestion is a device characteristic of Romantic poetry; some, like F. W. Bateson,[5] would even say it is peculiar to Romantic poetry and has no general application. The meaning that is suggested in Romantic poetry is diffuse, imprecise; the quality that enables a word or image to suggest such meaning is, to borrow Wimsatt's words again, 'the dreamy abstractness, the suffused vagueness of revery'.[6] Hulme's banner of revolt against Romanticism was the classicist principle of the accurate, the precise, the definite. Eliot seems to have taken over from the Romantic tradition its technique of suggestion and adapted it to classical values, evolving thus a new mode of suggestiveness that blends precision and control with range of reference and indirection.

> There is a time for the evening under starlight,
> A time for the evening under lamplight
> (The evening with the photograph album).
>
> ('East Coker')

We soon find that the poet has decided for us that in reading these lines we do not tend 'as when a pebble is dropped in a pool, to watch meanings opening out in rings'[7], but rather to 'determine the precise degree of evocation of particular figures'.[8]

The danger in substituting regulated richness of meaning for freely eddying meaning is that you can slip into one-to-one allegorical correspondence. This seldom happens in Eliot. There is, for instance, a carefully preserved difference between the three leopards of *Ash Wednesday* and the three beasts of the *Inferno*. The leopards have ordered associations of terror and beauty which are worked into the poem's structure, but they do not admit of equation with a concept. Eliot's vehicles have a directed significance, but nowhere are their tenors named.

In a sense, of course, 'controlled suggestion' is not a discovery to be credited to Eliot. It is rather the consummation of a tendency that inheres in the Symbolist method. One has only to look at pre-Symbolist romantic poetry or at automatic writing of any period to realize that before symbolism became a faith and a technique, the dreaming poet could think alogically and mythopoeically, and his symbols, being spontaneously created and unconsciously used, were non-rational and non-referential and possessed of portmanteau meaning. Once, however, the poet becomes aware that he is using symbols, he cannot use a symbol any more without it symbolizing (at least for him) something. The predicament of the Symbolist poet is just this: that a consciously used symbol is a contradiction in terms, in that it necessarily develops the finiteness of reference that is fatal to a symbol. No poet who knows that he is being suggestive can help suggesting something more or less definite! To look this dilemma in the face, as Eliot did, is not to slide from Symbolism into allegorizing or tenor-naming but to recognize that willed suggestion necessarily resolves itself into controlled and channelled release of multiple meaning.

It is significant that Lascelles Abercrombie, although a critic in the Romantic tradition, thought of suggestion as very much a contrived thing. He was led to this position not *via* the Symbolist *impasse* but by his notion of suggestion as secondary meaning. In the once influential essay, *Principles of Literary Criticism*, he says: 'In fact, literary language differs from ordinary language precisely by the conscious and deliberate use in it of powers additional to the force of grammatical meaning . . . Literary art, therefore, will always be in some degree *suggestion* . . . A very large part of literary skill consists in vividly liberating for its effect on imagination just that particular secondary meaning in words which is not only appropriate to the immediate occasion, but which will make the occasion come to life in the reader's mind.'

In order to watch 'controlled suggestion' at work and compare its mechanics with those of Romantic suggestion, we can place a stanza from the hymn in *Prometheus Unbound* alongside a stanza from the 'Little Gidding' lyric.

Life of Life! thy lips enkindle
  With their love the breath between them;
And thy smiles before they dwindle
  Make the cold air fire; then screen them
In those looks, where whoso gazes
Faints, entangled in their mazes.

*

Who then devised the torment? Love.
Love is the unfamiliar Name
Behind the hands that wove
The intolerable shirt of flame
Which human power cannot remove.
  We only live, only suspire
  Consumed by either fire or fire.

There are four images or terms—fire, love, life and breath
—common to the two stanzas; the way they work in each
is significant. In Shelley each term acts as a source of semantic
exhalation; and the terms are not encouraged to impinge
actively on one another. In Eliot, the same terms are found
moving by continual back-and-forth reference to one
another; they are placed in a specific if ambivalent relationship to each other of tension and confirmation, and they
simultaneously extend and define each other's meaning.
'Fire' in Shelley's line is meant to have unlimited resonance.
But as Yvor Winters once pointed out, maybe rather too
hard-headedly, our reaction to the word 'fire' would generally depend on whether the word as used on the occasion
relates to a fire on a hearth, in a furnace, or in a forest![9]
This defining power of context is active in Eliot's corresponding line. The two groups of associations that 'fire'
has—fire as desire that destroys and fire as purgatorial fire

that refines and redeems—are disposed there contrapuntally, and the second group is echoed and enriched by earlier lines in the lyric and indeed elsewhere in the poem. Certain associations of the word are thus selectively established, and the other associations are either excluded or muffled. The significance of 'love' is similarly defined by the references to divine grace in the context and earlier. 'Live' and 'suspire', operating in a way radically different from that of Shelley's 'life' and 'breath',[10] are in tension with 'consumed' in the next line, and this relationship determines their meaning. Indeed, the whole of *Four Quartets* is a system of interlocked symbols that release and regulate one another's meaning, demonstrating that suggestiveness can be reconciled with classical precision . . .

> Hung instantly upon the eyelashes, smote
> The lips, got shattered next on the high breasts,
> Ran down the stomach's stages—and at last
> The first drops of rain sank in her navel.
>> (From *Kumārasambhava*, an epic poem by Kālidāsa, the best known classical Sanskrit poet)

This chart of the raindrops' course is suggestive of Umā's beauty; each feature of it, long eyelashes, full lips, firm breasts—if these had not been such, the raindrops would not have behaved thus on each—answers perfectly to the traditional ideal. There is also a further suggestiveness here working through tension: the hinted loveliness of flesh is part of the picture of Umā in the erect attitude of the stern ascetic discipline whose object was the hermit god Śiva's love. Nothing can, on the face of it, be more different and distant from this than Eliot's picture in *Ash Wednesday*:

The broadbacked figure drest in blue and green
Enchanted the maytime with an antique flute.
Blown hair is sweet, brown hair over the mouth blown,
Lilac and brown hair . . .

Kālidāsa's lines are suggestive through their indirection,
Eliot's through their evocativeness. Kālidāsa's picture is
complete as far as it goes, though it has a significance
added to it; Eliot's is just three glimpsed details which call
up the whole vision. Yet one has only to compare the two
passages with Shelley's

> And wherever her aëry footstep trod,
> Her trailing hair from the grassy sod
> Erased its light vestige, with shadowy sweep . . .
>
> ('The Sensitive Plant')

to realize that the difference between Kālidāsa and Eliot is
less fundamental than the difference between Shelley and
Eliot. The suggestive power of Shelley's lines is the power
of n, and his images work by width and vagueness of reference. Kālidāsa's lines and Eliot's lines, on the other hand,
have a suggestiveness pointing to a finite unstated meaning
which, in the case of the pair of passages compared here,
happens to be the same: the beauty of the flesh seen against
a spiritual ascent that leads beyond it. The sense of such
beauty is expressed suggestively through its objective correlatives—the full lips and brown hair over them blown.

Using 'a set of objects' to 'evoke' a *particular* emotion'
(the phrases are from Eliot's well-known pronouncement
on the objective correlative) is a principle valid for all art.
What makes Eliot's formulation distinctive is its insistence
that the objects should be sensuously concrete and the

emotion-meaning particular. In much Romantic poetry neither the suggestive object nor the suggested meaning has definition. What Eliot was involved in was thus an experiment in taming the wild energies of suggestion and teaching it to be servant to the classical values of precise saying and finite meaning. This is what one might call 'classical suggestion', and there had been an experiment in it in a very much earlier and very different body of classical poetry and criticism, but Eliot clearly was not aware of this. He knew of ancient Indian philosophy—the *Upaniṣads*, the *Bhagavad-Gītā* and the Buddha's sermons—but as late as in 1955, writing to Nimai Chatterji, an Indian correspondent, he spoke of 'the author of *Vibhava* [*sic*], which I have not read'.[11] That he had no contact with Indian aesthetics only makes Eliot's experiment the more interesting.

It would, of course, be as absurd to liken Eliot's poetry to Kālidāsa's as to liken it to Virgil's. Kālidāsa's work—expressive of a simple untroubled vision, given to discursive narration, opulent in imagery—would indeed seem to be all that Eliot's is not. The point I am making is only that Eliot's poetry (of which his theory of the objective correlative was either a defence or an advance formulation)[12] and Kālidāsa's poetry (which, with other poetry of its kind, formed the basis of the Sanskrit theory of the objective correlative), while differing in all else, agree in adapting suggestion to classical values.

> Forthwith the *aśoka*'s boughs burst into shoot and blossom—
> He wouldn't wait till women's ankleted feet had touched him.
> (*Kumārasaṁbhava*)

These lines from Kālidāsa, on an untimely spring, can be set beside Eliot's lines on 'midwinter spring':

> Now the hedgerow
> Is blanched for an hour with transitory blossom
> Of snow, a bloom more sudden
> Than that of summer, neither budding nor fading,
> Not in the scheme of generation.
>
> ('Little Gidding')

The blossom of snow is part of a symbol, unusual rather than conventional, objectifying the 'stirring of the dumb spirit'. The *aśoka* blossom is similarly a detail in what is an extended objective correlative (a description of the spring, filling a sizeable portion of the canto) for 'the heart's heat' (to borrow Eliot's words) that disturbed the ascetic god Śiva when Umā appeared before him. Yet, while Eliot's image for the disturbance is the flaming ice acting on the soul's sap, Kālidāsa's image is the new-risen moon acting on the sea. The two images indicate the two widely disparate methods of objectification used by Eliot and Kālidāsa. Kālidāsa's objective correlatives are explicit, uncomplicated, sedately familiar when they are not merely ingenious. The *aśoka* flower, like all flowers, is a traditional *uddīpanavibhāva* ('stimulant-correlative') for love, and women's tread making the *aśoka* tree flower is a conventional idea. Nothing can be farther removed from the difficult condition or concept Eliot's lines are struggling to indicate.

Kālidāsa had the advantage of being born into a cultural closed system with a large fund of shared responses to objects so that within it the sensuous correlates of emotions for its members had a large measure of uniformity; he was also blest with membership of a poetic tradition which probably had already worked out a larger number of emotion-object relationships than most traditions do and had erected them into conventions. It was otherwise with

Eliot. The Elizabethans, and in a different way the Augustans, had the notion of an ideal order in nature and society to serve them as a frame of reference. The Romantics did not inherit a framework, but if they had inherited one, their commitment to the absolute sufficiency of the subjective principle would have ruled out any acceptance of external authority. Eliot's reaction against Romanticism was to evolve the concept of 'an ideal order' formed by 'the existing monuments' of 'the whole of the literature of Europe from Homer'. In submitting to the authority of this Christianized Graeco-Roman culture and the literary tradition it supported Eliot saw the answer to the anarchy and centrifugality of his own age and to all that repelled him in Romantic art. Their devotion to the ego and to the spontaneous overflow and the absence of an objective 'myth-kitty' made the Romantics employ arbitrary and personal symbols whose suggested meaning worked not by being widely and precisely recognized but by blurred reference and infinite diffusion. Eliot substitutes for this a method of allusion and quotation yielding symbols which, being drawn from tradition, combine range and reference with concreteness and precision and, having always been part of a system, are more amenable to control and direction. This surely is how the lady in the white gown of *Ash Wednesday* differs from the damsel with the dulcimer in *Kubla Khan* and the Arab maiden in *Alastor*. The images Eliot finds from English and European literature, Indian sacred literature, fertility myths and Christianity are easily identifiable within their own cultures which are accessible to all those who care, and because these images are public—because they indeed were the currency of thought and feeling in the past—they do not share the irresponsibility and unpredictability of private

symbols and are non-volatile and tractable where private
symbols tend to fade far away and dissolve. When Eliot does
use personal images, he ensures that they are so disposed as
to illuminate each other—or else he links them immediately
with known literary or religious lore and universalizes their
reference. Even if this is not done, a private image (according
to Eliot), if it is 'consciously concrete', will always become
'unconsciously general'. Conversely, in the hands of the
Romantics the hallowed images from mythology and nature
they sometimes used tended to get filled with a personal
meaning that transformed them beyond recognition.

The canto from which I quoted the lines about the
aśoka tree has a massing of the objective correlatives of love
—the mango and *karṇikāra* blossoms, the cuckoo sweet-
throated from eating the mango sprouts, the thirsty bee,
the creepers bent with bunches of flowers heavy as breasts,
Umā's girdle of flowers slipping from her waist, the glow
of perspiration on the *kimpuruṣa* women's bodies. Many of
these are conventional and stylized, maybe even stereotyped,
but exactly because they are the objects that tradition has
attached to the sexual emotion, they operate as precise and
potent suggestors of it. Indeed, an objective correlative is,
by definition, traditional—it is 'a specified, figuratively
fortified, and permanent object'[13] that literary tradition has
evolved for the corresponding emotion. Also, an objective
correlative works best in a classical climate—in an established
cultural situation where responses to the 'objects' are more
or less uniform and stabilized. The objective correlative is
thus an essentially classical device. Even C. K. Stead—
who is committed to the view that Eliot's theory and earlier
practice recognize 'unconscious process', and not 'conscious
direction', as the essential element in poetic composition—

identifies the objective correlative with the poem's willed structure which is the classical principle active in the poem.[14] (Eliot's belief, on Mr Stead's showing, is that what is most truly poetic in a poem has an inspirational or automatic origin; but Mr Stead accepts Eliot's view that 'there is a great deal, in the writing of poetry, which must be conscious and deliberate'[15]—like, for instance, the task of editing what has risen from below-conscious levels, or the technical tasks of craftsmanship. This is what I meant when I referred to Eliot's experiment as one in 'taming the wild energies of suggestion and teaching it to be servant to the classical values of precise saying and finite meaning'.) There has been another and more recent attempt—by Philip Le Brun— to show that 'Eliot's literary position cannot be called classical'.[16] Mr Le Brun discovers a Romantic basis for the objective correlative—the objective correlative, as he sees it, is the work of art itself, a direct and immediate presentation of the poet's perfectly fused thought and feeling. The poem, being thus a sensuous equivalent to an exceptionally inte-grated consciousness, embodies a special kind of insight. But this is closer to Bergson, Cassirer and Susanne Langer than to Eliot who meant by the objective correlative not the whole poem seen as a symbol but an individual image or set of images in it, such as, to reproduce Eliot's own example, the sensory details projecting the sleep-walking Lady Mac-beth's state of mind.

Clearly then, the objective correlative as conceived by Eliot is classical in nature and function. And suggestion, though generally a Romantic method, is, among other things, the business of evoking an emotion through its objective correla-tive. In this aspect, then, suggestion is a classical method. By developing the possibilities of suggestion in this direction and by attempting control and command of what used to be regarded as mindless and riderless, Eliot not only put suggestion to an unusual use but put himself in unusual company —the company of some dead masters whom he had not known.

9

Suggestion or Statement?
The Case of Wordsworth

Every time what looks like a symbol in Wordsworth beck-
ons me, I think of Patricia Beer's sonnet about him:

> Winter was not a symbol, nor was Spring,
> Nor was the corpse that floated to the air
> After a week of water, nor the wing
> Of the December star pinned to the mere
>
> By a child's skate. His dawns were literal,
> His ghosts did not melt from the ice of darkness
> But froze on into the sunshine. Guilt was real
> And the stern mountain had no other likeness.
>
> A lake was something that could drown him, though
> It danced, he said. The river had no voice
> Although it sang. He knew too well the plan
>
> By which the world shared neither grief nor joy
> And stood for nothing else, but really was
> The wet and dry, the hot and cold of man.[1]

Much has been written about Wordsworth's commitment
to the actual—a given thing was of interest to him because it
was what it was in itself. This is true enough, but a poet can
affect factualness on the surface while he transmits extra-literal
meaning at other levels. And even if his literalism is proved
to be genuine and pre-emptive of any intended symbolism

whatever, it need not invalidate the extended meanings that offer themselves when contact is made between poem and reader. This is theoretically the case. In practice, however, an object that the poet has elected to present naturalistically may not accommodate the kind of response that would treat it as a symbol, and then the quest for wider meaning soon enough runs into rough weather. David Perkins's attempt, for instance, to study the cottage girl in 'We are Seven' and the six-year-old in the 'Immortality Ode' as examples of the Romantic child symbol is blocked by the fact that both the children are presented as children in such realistic detail that to perceive anything at the level of symbol is made difficult by what is perceived at the more insistent level of fact, and Perkins is obliged to say, ' . . . there is a question whether the poem can be said to use a symbol'.[2]

That sea and mist, crag and torrent were symbols to Wordsworth in his life does not necessarily mean that they function as symbols in his poetry. Obviously, these are two different meanings of the word 'symbol'. An object or event that has been to a poet a felt symbol in life can be quite properly introduced by him in a poem to exist as a symbol in the latter sense. But a poet who, in doing so, describes it as a symbol and declares what it symbolizes is thereby interpolating the element of explication that precludes it from acting as a poetic symbol. The winds thwarting winds and the black drizzling crags on the slope of the Alps, which are described as 'symbols of Eternity', and the moon above Snowdon which is explicated at some length as 'the emblem of a mind', quite obviously do not even begin to be poetic symbols.

There is another sense in which the winds on the Alpine slopes cannot be symbols in the poem—they, like the loud

dry wind that roared in his ear as Wordsworth hung above
the raven's nest, are a real enough agent or factor of the
mystic experience, not a fictional counter of it as Dylan
Thomas's 'rocketing wind [that] will blow The bones out
of the hills' clearly is. When an object or event is conceived
as a component of reality and set in the cause-consequence
chain, its possibilities as a symbol are aborted. Once framed
in a rational context, it 'makes sense' in terms of itself and
of the context, and the compulsive need for a further meaning does not exist. A symbol, on the other hand, that is
not cause-linked becomes independent of the plot and free
to carry many-layered meaning. There is thus a qualitative
difference between 'The torrents shooting from the clear
blue sky' on Wordsworth's Alps, on the one hand, and on
the other, the piano set up by Madame Somebody on
Rimbaud's Alps and the 'flamingoes on the mountaintops at
dawn' in Karen Gershon's 'Swiss Morning'.

David Perkins—I return to him, as his is the most recent
considerable quest for symbols in Wordsworth—examining
the well-known 'Magnificent the morning' passage, speaks
of the obscure symbolic suggestion in the lines, arising, he
thinks, from the contrast between the sunrise on the
mountains (images of spirit) and the dawn in the meadows
and fields (images of the human).[3] One feels, however, that
the passage is no more than the record of an important
actual experience and owes its beauty to effects other than
symbolism. The high tones of the peaks and the subdued
light and the stir in the valley are what any Hollywood
camera, innocent of symbolism, would have picked out in
a contrastive sweep in the normal course. The occasion is
Wordsworth's dedication of himself to 'solitary study' and
'meditative peace'; the dawn, encountered in just the con-

ditions that would make its impact powerful, must have in actual fact caused (and maybe, being a dawn, also symbolized *to Wordsworth*) the commencement of a new life of single-minded submission to nature. In the poem it is far from a symbol—it is no more than a literal dawn.

The assumption that suggestion rather than statement is Wordsworth's central mode would have to be tested on those passages in his work which deal with experience that is most obstinately resistant to discursive presentation—on the great nodal passages, that is, of *The Prelude* which refer to his instants of illumination. Surely here, if nowhere else, Wordsworth would be driven to the use of symbol?

The apocalyptic passages that constitute the poetic core of *The Prelude* follow a more or less uniform pattern. There is first an explicit description of the situation that triggered the experience. The description ends abruptly and (one suspects) before it is complete, and a veil descends. And the next thing is a sonorous passage of apostrophe and philosophic musing. Between the two is the central hiatus—the moment itself, presented neither obliquely nor direct, indeed *presented* not at all, so that when the passage ends the secret is still inviolate. The mystical experience is led up to, hinted at, talked about, but nowhere is it presented either by suggestion or by statement. Consider, for example:

> ... the sky seem'd not a sky
> Of earth, and with what motion mov'd the clouds!

> The mind of Man is fram'd even like the breath
> And harmony of music. There is a dark
> Invisible workmanship ...

(I. 349–53)

But huge and mighty Forms that do not live
Like living men mov'd slowly through my mind
By day and were the trouble of my dreams.

Wisdom and Spirit of the universe!
Thou Soul that art the Eternity of Thought!

(I. 425–9)

. . . and I stood and watch'd
Till all was tranquil as a dreamless sleep.

Ye Presences of Nature, in the sky
Or on the earth! Ye Visions of the hills!

(I. 488–91)

And all the answers which the Man return'd . . .
Ended in this; *that we had cross'd the Alps.*

Imagination! lifting up itself
Before the eye and progress of my Song . . .

(VI. 521–6)

What we have in the text is the context and the doctrinal
comment—and both, though they cannot express the arcane
experience, keep talking about it. The experience is affirmed,
explained, commented upon in the poem, but it does not
happen within its language. The moment is not embodied
in the poem by 'sensuous re-creation'. This has resulted in
a general feeling that while the reality of Wordsworth's
mystical communion is undeniable, his way of expressing
it is that of a spectator. Archibald MacLeish sees this as the
difference between Rimbaud's visionary poetry and Wordsworth's: 'Where Wordsworth asserts the moment of insight
and tells us what the insight was—"Our birth is but a sleep
and a forgetting"—Rimbaud evokes the actual images in
which the insight exists.'[4]

Talking about the thing, expounding it propositionally,

or naming it, is Wordsworth's way not only with the clearly ineffable states but with all states of emotion.

Expressing an emotion is not the same thing as describing it. To say 'I am angry' is to describe one's emotion, not to express it. The words in which it is expressed need not contain any reference to anger as such at all. Indeed, so far as they simply and solely express it, they cannot contain any such reference . . .[5]

The words are Collingwood's, but they might well be Mammaṭa, the eleventh-century Indian critic, describing *svaśabdavācyatā* ('stating by its own name') which is the first in his list of *rasa-doṣa*s ('defects in the presentation of poetic emotion'). I wonder what Mammaṭa would have said about the statements in Coleridge's 'Dejection' where the emotion is identified and labelled and its symptoms recorded with clinical accuracy and directness. Certainly, Wordsworth's instinct seized upon statement as peculiarly suited both to his literalness and to his easy informative egotism.

Any study of Wordsworth's discursive method quickly develops into a study of his language—and here one has to compare, a process which, Wordsworth's status being what it is, involves comparing the greater with the lesser. Here are two pairs:

(1)   A motion and a spirit, that impels
       All thinking things, all objects of all thought,
       And rolls through all things.   ('Tintern Abbey')

       The force that through the green fuse drives the flower
       Drives my green age; that blasts the roots of trees
       Is my destroyer.
       And I am dumb to tell the crooked rose
       My youth is bent by the same wintry fever.
       (Dylan Thomas, 'The force that through the green fuse')

(2)   . . . Magnificent
   The morning was, a memorable pomp,
   More glorious than I ever had beheld.
   The Sea was laughing at a distance; all
   The solid Mountains were as bright as clouds,
   Grain-tinctured, drench'd in empyrean light.
                                    (*Prelude*, IV. 330–5)

   The point of one white star is quivering still
   Deep in the orange light of widening morn
   Beyond the purple mountains: thro' a chasm
   Of wind-divided mist the darker lake
   Reflects it: now it wanes: it gleams again
   As the waves fade, and as the burning threads
   Of woven cloud unravel in pale air:
   'Tis lost! and through yon peaks of cloudlike snow
   The roseate sun-light quivers.
                          (Shelley, *Prometheus Unbound*, II. i. 17–25)

One realizes how generalized the words 'motion' and
'spirit' are and how little work, apart from the alliteration,
'magnificent' 'memorable' and 'glorious' do. To describe
words of this kind (as R. A. Foakes does in *The Romantic
Assertion*) as 'value words' betokening man's highest hopes
and achievements or to argue (as G. C. Clarke does in his
Romantic Paradox) that Wordsworth uses words like 'form'
and 'shape' to express his sense of the essentially equivocal
nature of perception does not alter the fact that their suggestion potential is feeble. Wordsworth did often plump for
the non-thingy general word which, however 'lucid', can
only state where the sensuous image potently suggests.

   To take just one such word. 'Motion' occurs six times
within the space of 133 lines in Book I of *The Prelude*:

> sounds
> Of indistinguishable motion . . .
>
> (330–1)
>
> . . . and with what motion mov'd the clouds!
>
> (350)
>
> With measur'd motion, like a living thing . . .
>
> (411)
>
> a breath
> And everlasting motion . . .
>
> (430–1)
>
> spinning still
> The rapid line of motion . . .
>
> (481–2)

All the passages have reference to Wordsworth's flashes of insight. Returning to the theme seventy lines later, he returns to the same word:

> Those hallow'd and pure motions of the sense
>
> (551)

The word had already been used in the parallel statements of 'Tintern Abbey':

> And even the motion of our human blood
> Almost suspended . . .
>
> A motion and a spirit, that impels
> All thinking things . . .

Now it is clear that, whatever the word means in these lines, it does not mean 'movement'. When Wordsworth means movement plain and simple, he says movement:

> The coarser pleasures of my boyish days,
> And their glad animal movements all gone by.

It is equally clear that 'motion' does not mean the same thing in these passages. In expressing different if related experiences, not all of them equally capable of expression except obliquely through a suggestive image, Wordsworth must have found that 'motion', by its blurred outline and imprecise reference, was a useful alternative to image.

> When the stars threw down their spears,
> And water'd heaven with their tears ...
>
> ('The Tyger')

This is Blake's visionary sky. Confronted with a like apocalyptic transfiguration overhead, Wordsworth finds generality and tautology sufficient:

> the sky seem'd not a sky
> Of earth, and with what motion mov'd the clouds!

We can, of course, treat motion (as opposed to becalming or arrest) and spirit (identical originally with wind, breath, life) as archetypal images, as Maud Bodkin in fact does.[6] Or we might treat 'motion' as a word which Wordsworth uses in an idiosyncratic way, making it a carrier of a special or private meaning. What is more likely, however, is that the word, so inclusive in its non-sensuous indefiniteness, appealed to Wordsworth as offering a better approximation than most other words to the stir of strange energies around (and within) him. But (if we may apply to Wordsworth's words what Leavis said about his visionary moments), 'though Wordsworth no doubt was right in feeling that he had something to pursue, the critic here is in a different case!'[7] The plight of the critic or the reader has been described by Sir Maurice Bowra where he speaks of Wordsworth and Shelley talking about visionary experience in darkly abstract words. 'We see that something of utmost import is afoot and that the poet is transported outside his usual self, but we hardly know what has happened to him. The skies open, and he soars on the wings of inspiration to explore the infinite, but an impenetrable obscurity hides his goal from our eyes.'[8] This is probably overstating the case against words like 'motion', for no personal confession (whether direct or metaphoric) of mystic experience was ever free from obscurity. But it is true that when confronted with the mystical condition—a dark or dazzling but nonetheless concrete condition—Wordsworth generally used the abstract noun. To describe so specific and vivid an experience as the dissolution of the mind-matter disjunction (an experience he shook off as a boy by grasping a wall or a tree), Wordsworth (in the Fenwick note to the 'Immortality Ode') calls in a term from philosophical theory—'idealism'. And in the Ode itself, as he gets closer to the central mystery, he employs four gerunds in a row ('questionings', 'fallings', 'vanishings', 'misgivings') and then tries out a vivid image from *Hamlet* ('a guilty thing surprised'), only to revert the next moment to 'affections' and 'recollections'. The vocabulary of the notional is used to render the experiential. Wordsworth had taken over this vocabulary ('motion', 'presence', 'scene', 'fair', 'high', etc.) from the philosophy and poetry of the previous century. The nouns and adjectives of the eighteenth century generalize instead of discriminating, classify instead of specifying. As Donald Davie says, they 'turn their back upon sense-experience and appeal beyond it, logically, to known truths deduced from it'.[9] They are the instruments of thought of an age when 'nearly everybody thought that He (God) could be deduced by tracing laws and classes, not perceived in a leap of insight'.[10] Wordsworth, on the other hand, uses such words for rendering just such a leap of insight.

10

Suggestors of Emotion

The reaction against Bradley, inaugurated by L. C. Knights's broadside, 'How Many Children Had Lady Macbeth?', in 1933, seems to have run its course. We notice nowadays that the character-monger and the theme-pedlar are elaborately polite about each other's trades, and it is generally agreed that while characters are a part of the total design of the play, the design is not validated unless the characters are convincing 'persons'. On the one hand, Knights, whose powerful ridicule had almost stilled all talk about character, is now heard saying: ' . . . And I for one would rather see among my pupils an honest and first-hand appreciation of what is offered by way of "character" than a merely mechanical working out of recurrent imagery and symbolic situations.'[1] And for their part, the fine character studies and examinations of the character principle that we have had in recent years from John Bayley, John Harvey and others show that we have now a new generation of intelligent Bradleyans whose methods are much less vulnerable to the attack on character.

But not always. In *Milton's God*, Empson argues that Milton's Delilah is 'a high-minded great lady' and Milton's Samson an 'unintellectual' nihilist and braggart. I will say nothing here about the techniques of character analysis which led him to this conclusion; nor ask whether the conclusion is congruous with a poem which is a very conscious exercise in 'Tragedy, as it was antiently compos'd' and which is deeply personal, embodying (as Empson admits) a direct parallel to Milton's own life—because neither of these is my point here. My point is that Empson often gets away from the poem and into the Bible or into life.

Samson's statement to Harapha that his having married into the Philistine tribe the first time is proof of his goodwill is, Empson points out, disingenuous, since earlier on Samson had described the marriage as prompted by the Lord to enable him to find a *casus belli*. Empson's comment is:' . . . One might indeed argue that he is telling the truth now and was lying before, but the question is settled by Judges XIV. 4.'[2] But is it? Can anything in the Bible, can anything outside *Samson Agonistes*, settle whether the Samson of Milton's poem is mendacious here or not?

The second example concerns Delilah. Empson obviously likes her. His comment on her visit to Samson is: 'It would be wilful to doubt that she still loves him and wants to help him, because we are given no other reason for her visit.'[3] But we *are* given another reason—by Empson himself and in the very next sentence: 'She might indeed have a general political intention, to try to heal even now the divisions threatening civil war . . .'[4] Now where did Empson get that? From the poem? No—for he says later: 'And I grant, of course, that she does not express the aim of reconciling the two parties; that would exasperate Samson and at best sound a useless excuse to other people.'[5] When the text contains no evidence to support his guess, can the critic run up and fetch a reason from life or from the twilight realm of conditionals to explain away the absence of evidence? Is this Empson's alternative to the spatial-metaphorical approach and its 'inhumanity and wrong-headedness', as he once called it?[6] And if she had succeeded in her mission of love and peace and lived happily ever after with Samson, how many children would Lady Delilah have had?

No one, of course, would care to suggest today that what we know about a character should be no more than what the text explicitly tells us. But there is surely a difference between practising legitimate inference about a character and pursuing him down by-ways of speculation which lead away from the text. What the spell of the how-many-children game does to us is to make us forget that character is a function within the artefact's total being—what Knights today calls a 'vision of life—more or less complex and inclusive—whose meaning is nothing less than the *play as a whole*'[7] and formerly used to call (employing terms more like Richards's and less like Wilson Knight's) the 'system of values that gives emotional coherence to the play'.[8] Neither description would have surprised Sanskrit critics. They held, as we saw, that a poem is dominated by a cohesive principal emotion to which all the elements—plot, character, language—are more or less firmly oriented. (The dominant emotion is, of course, often amplified and diversified by the individual emotional motifs of the different scenes or episodes, and then a character may be aligned to the effect of the part, rather than the whole, of the play.) Characters thus are to be valued less for their individuality and verisimilitude than for their relevance to, and enrichment of, the total emotional pattern. This anti-naturalistic position offered no problem to a poetic developed partly from classical Sanskrit drama which was 'non-realistic, conditioned by conventions that helped to govern the total response obtained by means of the language of each play'.[9]

These are actually the words in which Knights describes Elizabethan drama. Which explains why his notion of the relation of character to the play's emotional nexus—a notion developed from Shakespeare's plays—is so similar to that of the Sanskrit critics. The distinction between the actual (*laukika*) and the aesthetic non-actual (*alaukika*), between *homo sapiens* and *homo fictus*, and the status of *homo fictus* as no more than a factor of the total emotional impression are true of all writing, but they are more obviously true of writing that employs conventions and symbols than of writing that doesn't. The debate about character in Shakespeare continues, I think, largely because we cannot agree on whether Shakespeare is naturalistic, or non-naturalistic, or both by turns. But the idea that character is an element in the pattern of the play as a whole and can have no independence or absoluteness is one that applies essentially to all drama and fiction, all along the scale from realism (such as Arnold Bennett's) to its opposite which we can take T. S. Eliot, among many others, as representing. It is significant that both of them agree about character—at least in theory. Arnold Bennett noted in his diary after a meeting with Eliot: 'I was thinking about what T. S. Eliot and I had said about character in fiction . . . It must somehow form part of the pattern, or lay the design of the book. Hence it must be conventionalized.'[10]

We found that Eliot's essay on *Hamlet* studies the Queen not as a human or quasi-human being but as the objective correlative—an inadequate one—of the essential emotion of the play and that Sanskrit critics would have viewed her in much the same way. In studying the balcony scene in *Romeo and Juliet*, they would have described Juliet's status and function there as similar to the moonlight's, both being the objective correlatives of love. This, we may feel, is pretty drastic. But if Juliet is the heroine (*nāyikā*) of the play, she is also, more importantly in the scene, the *ālaṁbanavibhāva* of love, one among the many *vibhāva*s of love concentrated in the scene. The only effective insurance against the how-many-children error is a firm hold on the essential status of character as an element in the play's emotional pattern. The naturalistic fallacy—the assigning of absoluteness and reality to characters—is, as we have seen, tenacious. And the *Rasa-dhvani* theory, precisely because it states so naïvely and coarsely that character, plot, imagery, rhythm and other elements have no *raison d'être* except as correlatives of emotion, can be uniquely serviceable as a prophylactic.

*   *   *

There are so many perceptive interpretations of *The Ancient Mariner* available now that it is tempting to get right back to Coleridge's own well-known account of what he meant the poem to be. This is perhaps going outside the evidence of the poem itself and attending to a mere spelling out of conscious intention, but it might all the same be a useful exercise:

... the incidents and agents were to be, in part at least, supernatural; and the excellence aimed at was to consist in the interesting of the affections by the dramatic truth of such emotions as would naturally accompany such situations, supposing them real ... it was agreed that my endeavours should be directed to persons and characters supernatural, or at least romantic; yet so as to transfer from our inward nature a human interest and a semblance of truth sufficient to procure for these shadows of imagination that willing suspension of disbelief for the moment, which constitutes poetic faith ... With this view I wrote the *Ancient Mariner* ...

We can, if we so choose, take the poet's statement at its face value and view the poem simply as a presentation of the marvellous. Walter Pater did so. The Sanskrit critics would have done so; they would have had no difficulty in identifying the ruling mood or emotion of *The Ancient Mariner* as *adbhuta* (wonder). To them *adbhuta* was linked with superhuman exploits (hence its special compatibility with the heroic emotion) and, what is more relevant to Coleridge's poem, with the intrusion of the supernatural. And curiously enough, if the Romantic movement of which *The Ancient Mariner* was an early flower has been called the Renascence of Wonder, Viśvanātha and other Sanskrit critics, speaking from classicist premises, also regard wonder as underlying all response to literature.

There is an important difference though: in that while in Sanskrit, the dominant emotion or mood of a poem or play is the mood that rules the central character, this can hardly be said to be the case in *The Ancient Mariner*. Neither the central figure nor any of his associates or final rescuers (except perhaps for the incomparable Pilot's boy) have adequately evident emotional responsiveness attributed to them. In the *Biographia Literaria* passage I have quoted, Coleridge talks about his formula for establishing credibility: which is, to interpolate in the poem realistic human emotional reactions. This is precisely what does not get done in the poem; the formula seems to have met with the same fate as Wordsworth's principle of reproducing the real language of men. Maybe the pace and dryness of ballad-style narration ruled it out; maybe inset naturalistic behaviour would have been incongruous. The experiences presented achieve credibility not by any infusion of naturalism but in the only way experiences in poetry can achieve credibility: by being made to happen within the language of the poem. Our assent, for instance, to the preternatural sights that greet the Mariner on awaking from his sleep is obtained not through the presentation of the beholder's sense of wonder but through the movement of the verse. 'The hundred fire-flags sheen',

> To and fro they were hurried about!
> And to and fro, and in and out,
> The wan stars danced between.

In the wind that was heard roaring but did not blow on the ship,

> ... the sails did sigh like sedge.

And the continuous cascading of the lightning is no more than a function of rhythm in the lines that describe it. The truth of these marvels is guaranteed for us by the language and not by the human witness's confession of wonder. The Mariner's report on these is utterly reticent about their impact on his mind, so that it is impossible to see him as the vessel of the poem's dominant emotion of wonder. This is true of the other characters as well, except, to be sure, for the Wedding-Guest, but he is outside the narrative.

Characters then are not objective correlatives of emotion in *The Ancient Mariner*. The burden of evoking the '*particular* emotion' of the poem (to use Eliot's terms again) is shifted from the 'set of objects' (whether men or spirits) to the 'chain of events'. The whole plot is organized round a unified final emotional impression, which is wonder. It is possible no doubt to study the story in other terms; for instance, as presenting a moral vision. This can indeed be treated as one level on which the story and imagery operate, although there are serious difficulties here, the chief of which is a structural one. With the return of love, prayer, sleep and rain and the falling off of the guilt badge, the sin-penance-redemption cycle is nearly complete before the first half of the poem is over, and the second half, on this showing, would be a gratuitous elongation of the final phase of the cycle. A moral concern there certainly is in the story, but to assume that the overt affirmations of it in the commentary or in the poem itself and the less overt intimations of the Christian imagery exhaust the significance of the poem or even that they establish the moral significance as the central one is to disturb the proportioning in the poem.

When looked at instead as the suggestor of the poem's essential emotion, the plot in its second half will be seen not as dragging tediously on but as justifying itself by its enrichment of the sense of wonder through a further chain of situations and images: the cloud-burst under a bright moon, with the stars dancing between the fire-flags sheen and the unbroken flow of lightning; the inspirited corpses, with the Mariner's knee touching his dead nephew's as the two of them pulled at the same rope; the seraph choir; the crimson shadows in the bay and the seraph forms on the deck; the sails of the returning ship as they appear to the hermit.

The second half of the plot thus continues and completes the objectification of the emotion of wonder. If valuing a poem merely or mainly for its embodiment of an emotion is too hedonistic an approach, it is at least justified by the results —viewed in these terms, the plot, as we found just now, moves easily into focus; and several logically inconsequential situations, which used to be explained away as dream work, are identified as material contributory to wonder. To read the poem thus is not to be like Goldsmith's school children ('And still they gaz'd and still the wonder grew'), for this

L

approach forces us to attend to the careful way the plot is so structured that the principal emotion as the directing force is maintained and yet (lest emotional unity should become the fourth Unity and a blight) is diversified and reinforced by means of ancillary emotions.

A modern poet would have risked touches of banality or even comedy in the poem with a view to that great antiseptic: irony. Coleridge, however, excluded anything that would be in conflict with wonder (except, as we will see, at the end), so that the wedding scene is strictly another world momentarily glimpsed and even the Mariner's reentry into solid familiar reality takes place in a hushed moonlit bay that looks more like dream than fact. So exclusively does the plot devote itself to the one emotion that the poem comes pretty close to being a monolithic rendering of it, the result, remarkably, being in this case not monotony but a rare concentration and tautness. A long poem needs a unifying emotion more than a short one does, but implicit in its length is the ineluctable fact that the emotion must ebb when it has flowed and that its diminution will have to be compensated. But in *The Ancient Mariner*, wonder never eases its pressure, so that the poem has an unremitting intensity characteristic of a lyric. It is like the preternatural lightning it celebrates:

> Like waters shot from some high crag,
> The lightning fell with never a jag,
> A river steep and wide.

Not that the poem is insulated from all emotions other than wonder. It does in fact have its moments of joy, loneliness, weariness, anguish, and, above all, fear. Fear is the emotion that recurs oftenest and combines best with wonder.

The wild aspect of the Mariner; the chilling sense of being pursued; the vision of the phantom ship; the dead crew assembled on the moonlit deck and mutely gazing—these and other moments of horror in the poem make the sinister and the macabre act upon and accentuate the purely marvellous.

But the crucial diversification of the central emotion is at the end of the poem. The reaching out of the Mariner's heart to 'Old men, and babes, and loving friends And youths and maidens gay', linking itself with a similar reaching out earlier to the 'happy living things' below the ship, is an emotional state that is basically alien to wonder. We might call it loving-kindness. We might call it, as McDougall did, the tender emotion. In Sanskrit, it approximates to *vātsalya*, the tenth *sthāyin*. A sense of the sweetness of common company or of the beauty of familiar creatures, offsetting the confrontation of the unusual and the weird— in this juxtaposition of contrapuntal emotions the design of the poem completes itself.

11

Notes on Suggested Meaning

EVALUATE IT, OR MERELY EXPLICATE?

In the well-known passage in *Seven Types of Ambiguity* where he analyses Nash's line, 'Brightness falls from the air', Empson lists all the meanings it suggests to him: the setting sun or moon; Icarus; the 'glittering turning things' mounted on the roofs of sixteenth-century buildings; hawks, lightning or meteorites descending on their prey; a bright earth under an overcast sky; static electricity from the hair; bright motes in sunbeams falling and becoming dust.[1] Elsewhere in the book Empson says: 'Most of the ambiguities I have considered here seem to me beautiful'[2]; and 'I should claim, then, that for those who find this book contains novelties, it will make poetry more beautiful.'[3] But is this claim true of his explanation of Nash's line? Can we be sure that all the meanings he has discovered are of aesthetic worth?

To be fair to Empson, he does concede that he has often omitted explicit aesthetic evaluation but adds that it always precedes or succeeds analysis. 'You think the poem is worth the trouble before you choose to go into it carefully, and you know more about what it is worth when you have done so.'[4] The same point is made by Wellek and Warren in their *Theory of Literature*: 'And sometimes the distinction is made between the "elucidatory" and the "judicial" as alternative types of criticism. But though separation between the exegesis of meaning (*Deutung*) and the judgement of value

(*Wertung*) can certainly be made, it is rarely, in "literary criticism", either practised or practicable . . . an essay which appears to be purely exegetical must, by its very existence, offer some minimal judgement of worth; and, if it is exegetical of a poem, a judgement of aesthetic worth . . . To spend time and attention on a poet or poem is already a judgement of value.'[5]

But saying, 'Well, we wouldn't be analysing the poem, would we, if we didn't think it worth it?' is only half the answer. The approval implied in the act of choosing a text for analysis is no more than a preliminary one and may be confirmed or withdrawn as exploration proceeds and contact is made with levels and areas of meaning. (Moreover, the thrills of exploration or the excitement of standing up for your own interpretation against your neighbour's can make you oblivious of the original question of the worth of the text. In fact the worth of the text soon seems proportionate to the number of meanings and patterns detected, so that conceivably the James Bond stories in which—mercifully facetiously—a wealth of archetypal imagery was recently discovered can take their place beside *The Ancient Mariner* and *The Waste Land*.) But distinct from an initial implied judgement of the value of the text, there is—or should be— another process of evaluation constantly at work during the analysis. Each time a fresh possibility of meaning offers itself, the critic should ask, 'But is this one poetic?' He should, of course, also ask, 'Does the context warrant it?' (if not 'Can the poet have intended that?') and possibly a few other questions too, but his paramount question would be, 'Is it aesthetically valuable?' If that is loaded or vague, we might frame the question the way Holloway does: ' . . . How much better does it make the actual passage? How much more shall we value that, enjoy it, feel it contributes notably to the play?'[6]

The influence and authority of the sciences have invested description with immense prestige and this, in literary studies, has been at the expense of evaluation. I began with *Seven Types* only because it is one of the earliest essays, and still the finest, in a mode—*explication des textes*—that has since acquired more and more vogue till today it has become the largest concern of criticism and scholarship. The larger the number of explicators and texts and the farther afield interpretation ranges, the less time and inclination it has for value judgements, so that the mere fact that a meaning can be, or has been, read into a text is now treated as conferring validity on it; whate'er is is right.

The temptation to fetch a meaning that does not (to use Empson's words) 'give the line its beauty' is the pitfall that awaits all verbal analysts, and this is something that Sanskrit critics of the ninth and subsequent centuries were very much alive to. To them, a further meaning assumed did not automatically qualify to be classed as 'suggested'. As we saw in Chapter 4, it is only when the exclusive importance of the further meaning is established that it can be treated as a case of 'suggestion'; and one of the factors of exclusive importance is superiority in aesthetic worth. If the additional meaning does not have greater beauty (*cārutva*) than the primary meaning, then it remains as merely additional meaning and the passage does not graduate to the rank of suggestive writing. It has second-class status and is graded as 'poetry of subordinate suggestion'. Although this sounds rather like quality control in industry, the approach has its merits. The distinction between what is beautiful and what is not was sharp in classical Sanskrit poetry as it indeed was in traditional literature everywhere, but it has broken down in our century. As C. Day Lewis says, 'for the modern poet nothing is inherently unpoetic simply because for the modern man nothing is inherently poetic . . .'[7] Precisely because that is so, the criterion of beauty, which Sanskrit poetics regarded as central to the exploration of unstated meaning, now becomes even more important in validating the meanings assumed by the explicator. And the principle of felt beauty can be an effective corrective to the increasing cerebrality in the experiencing of poetry which is reflected in the products of verbal analysis.

WHEN IS IT PARAPHRASABLE?

When is poetry paraphrasable and when is it not? Is poetry paraphrasable at all? The Symbolist doctrine is that poetry is, by definition, unparaphrasable (form and content being one), but critics subscribing to the doctrine are not above the temptation to paraphrase. The second half (beginning 'Who then devised the torment? Love.') of the 'Little Gidding' lyric can hardly be said to be in the discursive mode. Yet the lines have been reduced to a neat paraphrase by Mathiessen, one of Eliot's finest critics:

We can hardly face the fact that love is essentially not release but suffering; and that the intolerable burden of our desires—our Nessus Shirt—can be removed by nothing within our power, but solely through grace. All we have is the terms of our choice, the fire of our destructive lusts or the inscrutable terrible fire of divine Love.[8]

On the other hand, the Movement liked to define poetry as a kind of moral discourse and somewhat testily affirmed the legitimacy of paraphrase. But not all the Movement poets were always paraphrasable. Take, for instance, Elizabeth Jennings's lines on what men felt when Lazarus rose from the dead:

> This man was dead, I say it again and again.
> All of our sweating bodies moved towards him
> And our minds moved too, hungry for finished faith.
> He would not enter our world at once with words
> That we might be tempted to twist or argue with:
> Cold like a white root pressed in the bowels of earth
> He looked, but also vulnerable—like birth.

Obviously, paraphrasability is not always dependable as the badge of a tribe. Which brings us back to the question: When is poetry paraphrasable and when is it not?

According to Abhinavagupta, where it is an idea/fact (*vastu*) or a trope (*alaṁkāra*) that has been suggested, it can be expressed discursively as well; on the other hand, suggested meaning, when it is emotion, does not admit of statement. This is identical with the familiar position in Western theory that concepts are reducible to discourse and that untranslatable image is the only language of emotions. As a given shade or nuance of emotion that is being expressed is uniquely determined by the group of sensuous correlates discursively presented, it cannot be dissociated from them and expressed by any other means.

> Only one ship is seeking us, a black-
> Sailed unfamiliar, towing at her back
> A huge and birdless silence. In her wake
> No waters breed or break.
>
> (Philip Larkin, 'Next, Please')

The lines suggest that the only certainty for us is death. The metaphor that suggests the idea is easily resolved into literal statement—in fact, long before Larkin wrote them, the lines had already been paraphrased several times over by the moralizing poets of the eighteenth and earlier centuries ('Awaits alike the inevitable hour', etc.). A poem suggesting death not as an idea but as an emotive event would be very different:

> A widow bird sate mourning for her Love
>   Upon a wintry bough;
> The frozen wind crept on above,
>   The freezing stream below.
>
> There was no leaf upon the forest bare,
>   No flower upon the ground,
> And little motion in the air
>   Except the mill-wheel's sound.
>
> (Shelley)

The grey bleakness of the sense of death is evoked here by images of the external scene. The emotion, presented in these terms, cannot be done into any other terms.

> I am not yet born; provide me
> With water to dandle me, grass to grow for me, trees to talk
>   to me, sky to sing to me, birds and a white light
>   in the back of my mind to guide me.
>
> I am not yet born; forgive me
> For the sins that in me the world shall commit, my words
>   when they speak me, my thoughts when they think me,
>   my treason engendered by traitors beyond me,
>   my life when they murder by means of my
>   hands, my death when they live me.
>
> (Louis MacNeice, 'Prayer Before Birth')

The first verse, where the archetypal symbols of *joie de vivre* potently operate, is not paraphrasable. The second is. What it suggests is a concept rather than an emotion: the all-powerful determinism of society, and the individual's absolute involvement in its evil.

Of course, the distinction between concept and emotion should be handled cautiously. An idea or fact not touched with emotion is hard to come by in poetry, except in palpably descriptive or ratiocinative verse, and there it would invariably be stated, never suggested. Abhinavagupta, who emphasizes the difference between suggested emotion and all else suggested in point of paraphrasability, also emphasizes elsewhere that all suggestion of idea or trope terminates in the suggestion of emotion. In fact, the Larkin passage we looked at cannot be treated as presenting death as an arid concept—the idea of death certainly comes enveloped in feeling.

As we noticed in earlier chapters, when the suggested meaning is emotion, so instantaneously does it spring from the stated meaning (viz. from the objective correlatives) that the stages of the process—almost similar to the discharge of lightning—are imperceptible (*asaṁlakṣyakrama*). On the other hand, a fact or idea is, so to speak, more matter than energy, and suggesting it is a less rapid process whose steps are distinguishable (*saṁlakṣyakrama*). This speculative version of how meaning is formed can help to explain why what is suggested cannot be isolated and presented independently in the one case but can in the other. The theory cannot be claimed to be anything more than an insight and is offered here for what it is worth.

DEFINING IT, INSTEAD OF MUFFLING

> Sometimes
> on fogless days by the Pacific,
> there is a cold hard light without break
> that reveals merely what is—no more
> and no less. That limiting candour,
> that accuracy of the beaches,
> is part of the ultimate richness.
>
> ('Flying above California')

The quality of a lucid Californian day that Thom Gunn celebrates in these lines is also the quality of some of his poetry—certainly of large parts of the volume which accomplished his arrival in the full sense. That 'limiting candour', that defining overtness (with this important difference, that it is no part of richness of meaning, is not only no part of it but is basically alien to it) is a virtue he consciously practised in *The Sense of Movement* (1957). The poem 'Human Condition', which I examined in Chapter 6 as a case of suggesting a meaning only to 'de-suggest' or unfold it the next moment, is from *The Sense of Movement*. Image and explicated concept packed two-in-one fashion seems to have been the formula for most poems in this volume. Gunn's work has since gained so much in variety, suppleness and freedom that the mode of *The Sense of Movement* cannot be claimed to be his only, or even his characteristic, mode. Nevertheless, it might be rewarding to study it as an experiment in reversing the more common method which consists in muffling the tenor so that the vehicle is released from particularity of reference and its multiple meaning is enabled to operate as uninhibitedly as the contextual frame would let it.

'Round and Round', which I cited as the opposite of 'Human Condition' in method, is from Gunn's first volume, *Fighting Terms* (1954) and is typical of it. As the title implies, the poems present love and other themes largely in terms of fighting—through myths, that is, drawn from war and violence. The technique throughout is to offer the myth and avoid stating its import. Most of the myths are developed in some detail, even giving the impression of a one-to-one correspondence—but this is illusory, as their reference is imprecise and interpretable, and the poems are no more like allegories than the early Eliot is like Dante. The rewritten Achilles, Helen and Lazarus legends do point to something beyond themselves, but we are not quite sure to what. The reference of 'The Court Revolt', 'The Right Possessor' and 'Looking Glass' is less difficult to divine, and that of 'The Beach Head' still less difficult, but none of these poems is easy in the sense that it has a built-in explanation. Precisely this absence of a key makes *Fighting Terms* uniquely satisfying. 'The Secret Sharer', for instance, is a more convincing variation on the alter ego theme than 'The Monster' in the volume, *My Sad Captains* (1961)—more convincing because more reticent. In 'The Monster', Gunn is at pains to explain that the other self is a concretion of a ponderous consistency in love, luxuriating in bitterness and despair. The explanation inhibits the image.

The method of *Fighting Terms* got exchanged for its opposite in the next volume, *The Sense of Movement*. 'On the Move', in a way the title-piece and certainly the poem most typical of the volume, is a construct made up of declared image-concept equations.

They scare a flight of birds across the field:

The concept that this suggests is gratuitously set forth in the next line:

> Much that is natural, to the will must yield.

Another example:

> In goggles, donned impersonality.

The boys on motorcycles are

> The self-defined, astride the created will.

Similarly, in 'Thoughts on Unpacking', the 'sagging shapes', almost as soon as they are presented, are identified by the poet as traces of past tensions and errors which still cling to the lovers and imperil their relationship.

Weightless withered leaves rustling on the ground are the recurrent image in 'Autumn Chapter in a Novel'. Left to itself, it would have been an effective suggestor of the anaemic sentiment that brings the boy's languid mother and the tutor together. But Gunn insists on explicating the leaves as the lovers' words, sapless and ineffectual. The result soon enough becomes apparent. The poem moves to its climactic last line,

> And leaves thrust violently upon the pane

and precisely at the moment when the image must act with most energy, it is found to have lost much of its suggestive power. In fact, 'leaves' is now less an image than a nonce substitute term for 'words'.

Or take 'At the Back of the North Wind':

> . . . Other smells,
> Horses, leather, manure, fresh sweat, and sweet
> Mortality, he found them on the North.

The organic substances named here are between them quite adequate pointers to the North Wind being a symbol for mortal life. The explicit use of the word 'mortality' depresses the poem from the level of symbol to that of statement.

Gunn often gives in to a passion for abstract nouns like 'mortality' that reminds you of Wordsworth. He can, at times, use them with defiant ostentation—almost like a perverse child who seems to say, 'Look what I am doing!' In 'The Beaters', he places them where no one can miss them—as rhyme words, and they are complete with the morphemes that signal their abstractness. Thus: limitation, affectation, resignation, devastation; loneliness, gentleness; perversity, identity, liberty, extremity. The formal structure of the poem owes a great deal to these conceptual terms which bind each stanza together and round off ten out of the twenty-seven lines in the poem. The theme of 'The Beaters' —the inflicting and receiving of pain—is picked up again in the poem 'Innocence' in *My Sad Captains*; 'Innocence' offers the myth and leaves it at that. *The Sense of Movement* does include poems in this mode. If, for instance, 'The Inherited Estate' can be read as a gracious compliment to American culture, it is because the two dominant images—the follies and the young tree—are allowed to work unaided. This, however, is a departure from the prevailing manner of the volume, which is to define and explicate suggested meaning, thus transferring it from the potential to the actual level and ensuring (to borrow Gunn's words from a different context) that our perception

> rests on the things,
> and is aware of them only in
> their precise definition, their fine
> lack of even potential meanings.
> ('Waking in a Newly-built House')

When Gunn's imagery is described as precise, what is meant is apparently not that it is sharp and vivid (in fact Gunn's poetry is conspicuously non-sensuous) but that each image has a reference that can be particularized and is in fact particularized in the poem in so many words. As to what made Gunn elect this mode for the best part of *The Sense of Movement*, one can only guess. Possibly, the increased philosophic commitment obliged him initially to point up the concept each time. Possibly, in the case of some poems, his allegiance to the Movement inclined him to explicitness. This is mere speculation; what is clear from his subsequent work is that he soon ceased to be a prisoner of the image-plus-spelled-out-tenor formula, although he returns to it at will.

To look at *Fighting Terms* and *The Sense of Movement* as we have done, solely in terms of whether the tenor is stated or omitted, helps to account for the curious divergence in the critical responses to Gunn's early work. Alan Brownjohn, for instance, complains of the obscurity of *Fighting Terms*: ' . . . the themes and the nature of the poet's thinking were frequently muffled by the over-elaborate metaphysical conceits . . . Many of the poems in *Fighting Terms* are very similar: the manner and invention exciting, the import muffled and vague because of the means employed . . .'[9] John Press, on the other hand, admires the lucidity of the title-piece of *The Sense of Movement*: 'Gunn develops a complex metaphysical argument through a series of images which are exact symbols for certain emotional states and intellectual concepts.'[10] Both are, of course, right. Only, Mr Brownjohn's blame is in effect praise and Mr Press's praise blame. Muffle the import is precisely what poetry ought to be doing. And an exact symbol is at best a poor symbol.

DISOWN IT AND/OR DISPLAY

Robert Graves's poem, 'Turn of the Moon', tells how it is the
moon 'as she turns' that brings all rain:

> But if one night she brings us, as she turns,
> Soft, steady, even, copious rain
> That harms no leaf nor flower, but gently falls
> Hour after hour, sinking to the tap roots,
> And the sodden earth exhales at dawn
> A long sigh scented with pure gratitude,
> Such rain—the first rain of our lives, it seems,
> Neither foretold, cajoled, nor counted on—

such rain, adds suddenly the next line which is the last line
of the poem,

> Is woman giving as she loves.

This is essentially the same as Thom Gunn's method in
The Sense of Movement, but it works in an altogether different way. When the suggested meaning is dramatically
revealed in the last line (the effect being recognition no less
than surprise), the line proceeds to react on the body of the
poem, flooding it with a new, a human, meaning. The
effect thus is enrichment, because the tenor that Graves
makes explicit is not a concept but the human term of the
image.

A piquant variation of this method is to offer the suggested
meaning with innocent-seeming openness, prefacing it with
a palpable announcement; as much as to say, 'N.B. The
suggested meaning is as follows'. Vernon Scannell tries this
out in 'Incendiary':

> That one small boy with a face like pallid cheese
> And burnt-out little eyes could make a blaze
> As brazen, fierce and huge, as red and gold
> And zany yellow as the one that spoiled
> Three thousand guineas worth of property
> And crops at Godwin's farm on Saturday
> Is frightening, as fact and metaphor:

The facts having been set forth, the promised explanation of what they symbolize is appended:

> And frightening, too, that one small boy should set
> The sky on fire and choke the stars, to heat
> Such skinny limbs and such a little heart
> Which would have been content with one warm kiss,
> Had there been anyone to offer this.

George Barker's 'A Sparrow's Feather' is an experiment in another, and more provocative, refinement of the tenor-naming technique. Offer a compulsively suggestive image, and as you do so, solemnly warn all concerned that it means no more than it says. Barker tells how a young sparrow came and died in an empty birdcage which he had filled with birds of glass and paper and tin bits. The poem ends:

> So there, among its gods,
> that moaned and whistled in a little wind,
> flapping their paper anatomies like windmills,
> wheeling and bowing dutifully to the
> divine intervention of a child's forefinger,
> there, at rest and at peace among its monstrous
> idols, the little bird died. And, for my part,
> I hope the whole unimportant affair is
> quickly forgotten. The analogies are too trite.

M

The first part of R. S. Thomas's sonnet 'From Home' is an account of how when people return from the high pastures in Wales to the towns, the soil full of grass seeds is transferred from their boots to the cracks in the pavement and puts out grass in due course. The poem continues:

> There is no meaning between these lines.
> I am not thinking of mixture of race
> Or earth's abundance . . . And yet, and yet:
> The perpetual current of Welsh feet
> Watering these grasses, addressed in vain
> To the late greenness of their hearts!

First disown, then display—here is a combination of the two modes that is an advance on either. A statement of suggested meaning is redeemed by a show of naïve frankness. It is more than redeemed, it acquires a sophistication that positively justifies it, when it is prefaced with a tongue-in-the-cheek denial that there is any suggested meaning whatever.

We had in earlier chapters made it look almost like a doctrine that what has been suggested cannot then be stated without damage to the poem. If this is true as a general principle, the virtuosity of some contemporary poetry does establish that it is only true as a general principle and that there can be departures that more than justify themselves by their charming disingenuousness and by their daring.

THE NOT-GIVEN

Omission must have originated as a taboo in primitive communities which feared that the naming of certain things or people would bring ill luck. From a superstitious practice it developed in due course into a philosophical concept. Early

Indian philosophy and logic, noting that the total meaning
of a sentence is more than the sum of the meanings of its
constituent words, assumed that since the extra meaning
was conveyed by the relations between the words and not
by the words themselves, it could be said to have been
conveyed by suppression as distinguished from expression.
Neither the truth of this theory nor whether this notion of
suppression in conveying a judgement is the same as the
notion of poetic meaning being suggested instead of being
expressed is of interest to us here. It is the latter notion by
itself—poetic suggestion by omission—that concerns our
enquiry, and we find it occurring in the ninth-to-eleventh-
century Sanskrit criticism that we have been constantly
referring to, where we have critics speaking of matter being
presented through concealment (*samvṛttyābhihitam*—Ānandavardhana) and attaining beauty through concealment
(*gopyamānatayā labdhasaundaryam*—Abhinavagupta). 'In a
symbol,' as Carlyle said much later, 'there is concealment
and yet revelation: hence therefore, by Silence and by
Speech acting together, comes a double significance.' By
the end of the nineteenth century this was a familiar principle
in Western thinking. As we saw in an earlier chapter,
Whitman, writing in 1888, declared that he rounded and
finished little; eight years later, Santayana spoke of the
study and enjoyment of 'the suggestion of the not-given,
rather than the form, the harmony of the given'.[11] Now if
this was, as he called it, 'the evident characteristic of modern
genius' in Santayana's time, it is more so in ours. Silence as a
language is an influential cult today, and a blank page, we
are assured, is the perfect poem.

To be sure, explication of the suggested meaning (as
we saw in previous chapters and further in this chapter) does

affect the quality of a poem. But if there is anything more injurious to a poem than thorough explication of the tenor, it is thorough suppression of it. Complete omission of the tenor involves not only leaving it unnamed but also providing no hints or pointers in its direction, with the result that all reference is drained off from the representational content of the poem which then lies inert, asking nothing, offering nothing. Partial omission has the opposite effect— it makes the poem come alive. It can take the form of fragmentary statement that leaves you restless; it can also take the form of suggested meaning that is half-revealed so that a compulsive need for apprehending the rest is generated and various competing possibilities of meaning knock on the door. The reader's imagination is soon working full throttle. This cannot happen when none of the suggested meaning is revealed, nor when all of it is.

Take, for instance, John Holloway's poem, 'Beast of Burden':

So 'Let me help!' you twitter: and you make
Gingerly as if to . . . then, quick, you let me slump
Off-balance on the ground. And, 'Why doesn't my back break?'
You complain, and you gawk at the great hang-dog hump
That bouldered all the door-jambs as I groped
Into your house. Why this grotesque back-lash
(You ask) I sweat so much to get roped,
Knotted onto me? Use a gully! Slash!
Well . . . would you really have me fling away
My millstone, stoneself, self break counterpart?
Don't they bury men whose crime is felo-de-se
At those coloured lights? Drive a faggot through the heart?
Better look twice, hadn't you, at my pack,
See what it is drowsing on my back.

Except for a hint or two, offered in the words 'the great hang-dog hump' and 'drowsing', the burden on the back is a sinister mystery screened from view. The minimal nature of the representation ensures that no more than an incipient image of what is carried on the back results. If the picture were complete, its very roundedness and clarity would lower its suggestive potency.

If the vehicle is thus partially presented, the tenor is glimpsed very faintly indeed. The glimpse is afforded in the line,

My millstone, stoneself, self break counterpart.

This says enough, if only just enough, to energize the reader's imagination and make it work out what is not said. If the line were removed, the poem would be an exercise in total suppression and inarticulate to the point of self-extinction. And if, on the other hand, the line were to be rewritten in the motorcycle = created-will manner, the poem would extinguish itself in a different way.

Omission is the very condition of the reader-participation aspect of suggestion. And never was this function better described than by Dryden in 'The Dedication of the Georgics' (1697):

I must confess the Criticks make it one of *Virgil's* Beauties, that having said what he thought convenient, he always left somewhat for the imagination of his Readers to supply: That they might gratifie their fancies, by finding more, in what he had written, than at first they cou'd; and think they had added to his thought, when it was all there before-hand, and he only sav'd himself the expence of words.

It is ironical that this almost definitive account of how omission works in suggestive writing should be offered by a master of non-suggestive poetry.

NOTES

I. SUGGESTION TODAY

1 W. Empson, *Seven Types of Ambiguity* (London 1930), pp. 63–4.
2 C. Brooks and R. P. Warren, *Understanding Poetry* (New York 1938/1966), pp. 379–80.
3 E. M. W. Tillyard, *Poetry Direct and Oblique* (London 1945/1959), p. 29.
4 W. Righter, *Logic and Criticism* (London 1963), pp. 87–116.
5 I. A. Richards, *The Philosophy of Rhetoric* (New York 1936/1950), p. 40.
6 W. Empson, op. cit., p. 1.
7 E. M. W. Tillyard, op. cit., p. 84.
8 W. K. Wimsatt Jr., *The Verbal Icon* (New York 1954), p. 109.
9 T. S. Eliot, *Selected Essays* (London 1932), p. 300.
10 R. P. Blackmur, *Language as Gesture* (London 1954), p. 6.
11 Ibid., p. 19.
12 Ibid., p. 16.

2. SUGGESTION: FROM POE TO THE PRESENT

1 The Oxford English Dictionary, under 'Suggest' 3.
2 See F. W. Bateson, *English Poetry and English Language* (New York 1961), p. 52.
3 D. Perkins, *Wordsworth and the Poetry of Sincerity* (Cambridge, Massachusetts/London 1964), p. 100.
4 See D. G. Hoffmann (ed.), *American Poetry and Poetics* (New York 1962), p. 254.
5 See D. G. Hoffmann (ed.), op. cit., p. 318.
6 J. Isaacs, *The Background of Modern Poetry* (London 1951), p. 19.
7 A. D. Hope, *The Cave and the Spring* (Adelaide 1965), p. 7.
8 A. C. Bradley, *Oxford Lectures on Poetry* (London 1909/1926), p. 26.
9 W. B. Yeats, *Essays and Introductions* (London 1961), p. 161.

10 H. Read, *Phases of English Poetry* (London 1928), p. 122.

11 L. Abercrombie, *The Idea of Great Poetry* (London 1925), p. 19.

12 L. Abercrombie, *Principles of Literary Criticism* (London 1932/Bombay 1958), p. 38.

13 T. S. Eliot, *Selected Essays*, pp. 300, 315.

14 F. W. Bateson, *English Poetry, a Critical Introduction* (London 1950/1966), p. 20.

15 W. K. Wimsatt Jr., *The Verbal Icon*, p. 146.

16 J. Bayley, *The Romantic Survival* (London 1957), p. 189.

17 O. Barfield, *Poetic Diction* (London 1928), p. 133.

18 W. J. Bate (ed.), *Criticism: the Major Texts* (New York 1952), p. 183.

19 D. Perkins, op. cit., p. 100.

3. SUGGESTION THROUGH THE OBJECTIVE CORRELATIVE

1 T. S. Eliot, *On Poetry and Poets* (London 1957), p. 152.

2 H. Levin, *Contexts of Criticism* (Cambridge/Massachusetts 1958), p. 259.

3 See F. Kermode, *Romantic Image* (London 1957), p. 150.

4 T. S. Eliot, op. cit., p. 26.

5 T. S. Eliot, *Selected Essays*, p. 51.

6 W. K. Wimsatt Jr., *The Verbal Icon*, p. 38.

7 T. S. Eliot, op. cit., pp. 144-6.

8 A. B. Keith, *The Sanskrit Drama* (London 1924), pp. 276-7.

9 W. McDougall, *An Outline of Psychology* (London 1923/1949), p. 324.

10 R. Skelton, *The Poetic Pattern* (London 1956), p. 7.

11 K. Smidt, *Poetry and Belief in the Work of T. S. Eliot* (London 1949), p. 110.

12 F. O. Mathiessen, *The Achievement of T. S. Eliot* (New York 1935), p. 63.

13 W. K. Wimsatt Jr., op. cit., p. 37.

14 G. Hough, *Image and Experience* (London 1960), p. 17.

15 R. Williams, *Drama from Ibsen to Eliot* (London 1952), p. 17.

16 I. A. Richards, *Principles of Literary Criticism* (London 1934), pp. 290, 293.

4. THE LAMP AND THE JAR:
STATED AND SUGGESTED MEANING

1 I. A. Richards, *Speculative Instruments* (London 1955), p. 41.
2 Ibid., p. 54.
3 D. Davie, *Articulate Energy* (London 1955), p. 21.
4 T. S. Eliot, *The Use of Poetry and the Use of Criticism* (London 1933), p. 151.
5 F. W. Bateson, *English Poetry, a Critical Introduction*, p. 19.
6 J. Bayley, *The Romantic Survival*, p. 220.
7 T. S. Eliot, op. cit., pp. 152-3.
8 J. Bayley, op. cit., p. 217.
9 E. M. W. Tillyard, *Poetry Direct and Oblique*, pp. 11-14.
10 W. Empson, *Seven Types of Ambiguity*, p. 62.
11 L. Abercrombie, *Principles of Literary Criticism*, pp. 39-40.
12 T. S. Eliot, *Selected Essays*, p. 299.
13 Ibid., p. 145.
14 Ibid., p. 300.
15 F. W. Bateson, op. cit., p. 20.
16 J. Bayley, op. cit., p. 219.
17 F. W. Bateson, *English Poetry and the English Language* (London 1950), pp. 42-3.
18 Quoted in R. Skelton, *The Poetic Pattern*, p. 49.
19 W. Empson, op. cit., p. 26.
20 C. Brooks and R. P. Warren, *Understanding Poetry*, p. 106.
21 W. B. Yeats, *Essays and Introductions* (London 1961), p. 160.
22 C. Brooks and R. P. Warren, op. cit., p. 341.
23 W. Y. Tindall, *The Literary Symbol* (Bloomington 1955), p. 19.

5. SUGGESTION THROUGH METAPHOR

1 C. Brooks, *Modern Poetry and the Tradition* (London 1948), p. 22.
2 C. Day Lewis, *The Poetic Image* (London 1947), p. 54.
3 A. Tate, *The Man of Letters in the Modern World, Selected Essays: 1928-1955* (New York 1955), pp. 64-77.
4 I. A. Richards, *Principles of Literary Criticism*, p. 240.
5 W. K. Wimsatt Jr., *The Verbal Icon*, p. 127.

6 A. MacLeish, *Poetry and Experience* (London 1961), p. 65.

7 I. A. Richards, op. cit., p. 240.

8 F. W. Bateson, *English Poetry, a Critical Introduction*, pp. 44–52.

9 H. Read, *Phases of English Poetry*, p. 127.

10 C. Brooks and R. P. Warren, *Understanding Poetry*, pp. 321–2.

11 W. B. Stanford, *Greek Metaphor: Studies in Theory and Practice* (London 1936), p. 101.

12 I. A. Richards, *The Philosophy of Rhetoric*, p. 127.

13 W. K. Wimsatt Jr., op. cit., p. 127.

14 W. Empson, *The Structure of Complex Words* (London 1951), pp. 333–4, 341.

15 See also K. Kunjunni Raja, *Indian Theories of Meaning* (Madras 1963), p. 266.

16 A. Tate, op. cit., pp. 76–7.

17 C. Brooks and R. P. Warren, op. cit., p. 364.

18 C. Day Lewis, op. cit., pp. 93–5.

6. STATING AND SUGGESTING BY TURNS

1 E. M. W. Tillyard, *Poetry Direct and Oblique*, pp. 11–15.

2 D. Davie, *Purity of Diction in English Verse* (London 1952/1967).

3 C. Day Lewis, *The Poetic Image*, p. 94.

4 J. Bayley, *The Romantic Survival*, p. 124.

5 T. S. Eliot, *On Poetry and Poets*, p. 26.

6 Ibid., p. 32.

7 Ibid., p. 74.

8 Ibid., p. 32.

9 Ibid., p. 76.

7. STATEMENT POETRY

1 E. M. W. Tillyard, *Poetry Direct and Oblique*, p. 10.

2 W. K. Wimsatt Jr., *The Verbal Icon*, p. 237.

3 L. Abercrombie, *The Idea of Great Poetry*, p. 49.

4 D. Davie, *Purity of Diction in English Verse*, p. 68.

5 Susanne K. Langer, *Feeling and Form* (London 1952), p. 223.

6 J. Wain (ed.), *Interpretations* (London 1955), p. 204.

7 T. E. Hulme, *Speculations* (London 1924), pp. 134–5.

8 F. W. Bateson, article on 'The Language of Poetry' in *The Times Literary Supplement* of 27 July 1967.

9 V. de S. Pinto and W. Roberts (ed.), *The Complete Poems of D. H. Lawrence*, vol. 1 (London 1964), p. 27.

10 Ibid., p. 28.

11 Ibid., p. 28.

12 Ibid., p. 184.

13 Quoted from one of D. H. Lawrence's letters in F. O. Mathiessen, *The Achievement of T. S. Eliot*, p. 89.

14 V. de S. Pinto and W. Roberts (ed.), op. cit., p. 27.

15 P. Larkin, review of John Betjeman's *Collected Poems* in *Listen* (Spring 1959), pp. 14–22.

16 T. S. Eliot, *On Poetry and Poets*, p. 32.

17 Ibid., p. 74.

18 Quoted from an unpublished lecture (1933) in F. O. Mathiessen, op. cit., p. 90.

19 T. S. Eliot, *On Poetry and Poets*, p. 82.

20 Ibid., p. 74.

21 R. Williams, *Drama from Ibsen to Eliot*, p. 239.

22 T. S. Eliot, *On Poetry and Poets*, p. 77.

23 C. Brooks, *Modern Poetry and the Tradition*, p. 112.

24 Ibid., p. 116.

8. SUGGESTION AS A CLASSICAL METHOD

1 J. Bayley, *The Romantic Survival*, p. 192.

2 W. K. Wimsatt Jr., *The Verbal Icon*, p. 150.

3 F. W. Bateson, *English Poetry, a Critical Introduction*, p. 20; W. K. Wimsatt Jr., op. cit., p. 147; T. S. Eliot, *Selected Essays*, p. 326.

4 T. S. Eliot, *Selected Essays*, p. 326.

5 F. W. Bateson, *English Poetry*, pp. 20–21.

6 W. K. Wimsatt Jr., *The Verbal Icon*, p. 144.

7 G. S. Fraser, 'Approaches to *Lycidas*' in *The Living Milton*, ed. F. Kermode (London 1960), p. 50.

8 L. C. Knights, *Explorations* (London 1946), p. 16.

9 Y. Winters, *In Defence of Reason* (Denver 1937/1943), p. 363.

10 See F. W. Bateson's article on 'The Language of Poetry' in *The Times Literary Supplement* of 27 July 1967, where he classes 'breath'

among 'the much too emotionally suggestive words' that modern
poetry tends to avoid.

11 Reproduced in the *New Statesman* of 5 March 1965.
12 T. S. Eliot, *On Poetry and Poets*, p. 26.
13 W. K. Wimsatt Jr., op. cit., p. 37.
14 C. K. Stead, *The New Poetic* (London 1964), p. 130.
15 T. S. Eliot, *Selected Essays*, p. 21.
16 See Philip Le Brun's article on 'T. S. Eliot and Henri Bergson'
in *Review of English Studies* (August 1967), p. 285.

9. SUGGESTION OR STATEMENT?
THE CASE OF WORDSWORTH

1 *P.E.N. New Poems 1960* (London 1960), p. 24.
2 D. Perkins, *The Quest for Permanence* (Cambridge, Mass. 1965), p. 75.
3 Ibid., p. 47.
4 A. MacLeish, *Poetry and Experience*, p. 170.
5 R. G. Collingwood, *The Principles of Art* (London 1938), p. 111.
6 M. Bodkin, *Archetypal Patterns in Poetry* (London 1934), pp. 30–6.
7 F. R. Leavis, *Revaluation* (London 1959), p. 174.
8 C. M. Bowra, *The Romantic Imagination* (London 1950), p. 277.
9 D. Davie, *Purity of Diction in English Verse*, p. 48.
10 Ibid., pp. 41–2.

10. SUGGESTORS OF EMOTION

1 L. C. Knights, *Further Explorations* (London 1965), p. 203.
2 W. Empson, *Milton's God* (London 1965), p. 216.
3 Ibid., p. 220.
4 Ibid., p. 220.
5 Ibid., p. 222.
6 W. Empson, article on 'Hunt the Symbol' in *The Times Literary
Supplement*, 23 April 1964, p. 339.
7 L. C. Knights, *Further Explorations*, p. 190.
8 L. C. Knights, *Explorations*, p. 47.
9 Ibid., p. 5.
10 Miriam Allott, *Novelists on the Novel* (London/New York 1959),
p. 290.

II. NOTES ON SUGGESTED MEANING

1 W. Empson, *Seven Types of Ambiguity*, p. 26.
2 Ibid., p. 235.
3 Ibid., p. 256.
4 Ibid., p. xiii.
5 R. Wellek and A. Warren, *Theory of Literature* (New York 1949), p. 250.
6 J. Holloway, *The Charted Mirror* (London 1960), p. 208.
7 C. Day Lewis, *The Poetic Image*, p. 106.
8 F. O. Mathiessen, *The Achievement of T. S. Eliot*, p. 191.
9 A. Brownjohn in *The London Magazine* for March 1963, p. 46.
10 J. Press, *Rule and Energy: Trends in British Poetry since the Second World War* (London 1963), p. 193.
11 G. Santayana, *The Sense of Beauty* (New York 1896), p. 174.

INDEX

179